THIS FAR BY FAITH
American Black Worship and Its African Roots
is dedicated to the memory of
Aubry Felix Osborn, 1922-1973,
priest of New Orleans and of Baton Rouge,
by his friend, H. Suzanne Jobert,
whose gift has enabled its preparation and first printing
as a joint publication project of
The National Office for Black Catholics
and The Liturgical Conference.

The essays which comprise this volume were originally addresses
delivered at a conference on *Worship and Spirituality in the
Black Community,* February 18-20, 1977, sponsored by the
Department of Culture and Worship of The National Office for
Black Catholics, in consultation with the Bishops' Committee
on the Liturgy and the Center for Pastoral Liturgy, held at
The Catholic University of America and St. Benedict the Moor
Parish, Washington, D.C.

Verbatim transcripts of the addresses were edited by Robert W. Hovda
and corrected or approved by the authors.

Design by David Camele, Loveland, Ohio

ISBN 0-918208-05-X
Library of Congress Catalog Card Number 77-89744
© 1977 by The Liturgical Conference, Inc. All rights reserved.
Printed in the United States of America

The Oral African Tradition Versus the Ocular Western Tradition:
© 1976 by Clarence Jos. Rivers

Front cover: From an original woodcut print,
Here Comes that Pentecost Again by David Camele

THIS FAR BY FAITH
American Black Worship and Its African Roots

Published jointly by:
The National Office for Black Catholics
1234 Massachusetts Ave., N.W.
Washington, D.C. 20005
and
The Liturgical Conference
1221 Massachusetts Ave., N.W.
Washington, D.C. 20005

CONTENTS

IN MEMORY OF AUBRY F. OSBORN, 1922-1973

"Sing your song, child!"

In his address at the conference which this book records, Henry Mitchell used a phrase to illustrate a Black cultural insistence on the priority of the person over institutions, forms and things. The phrase, commonly heard as a spontaneous expression in Black worship assemblies, is "Sing your song, child!" The emphasis is on *your*. You cannot sing that song as it deserves to be sung, unless you make it your own, unless you feel free with it, unless you bring your whole self to it, unless you contribute to it your own gifts and make a new creation out of what composer and lyricist have done.

This is a book to delight the heart of Aubry Osborn, to whose memory it is dedicated and whose long-time friend, H. Suzanne Jobert, has enabled its publication. Because this content goes way beyond familiar pleas for understanding, tolerance, respect and integration. Those pleas served a certain stage, a primitive stage of our recovery, or our development. But every day is new and, despite the terrible burden of our past, perhaps now we can begin to hear what these authors are saying about a wider discernment of and benefit from the beauty and the gifts of the Black cultural-spiritual tradition.

Aubry Felix Osborn was a native of New Orleans, born (of Leona Rousseve and Aubrey J.) and baptised in 1922, the fourth of seven children in a family whose closeness was to offer much needed support. After high school he determined he would seek to serve in the church's presbyterate, and to that end he was willing to repeat his secondary education at St. Augustine's Seminary, Bay St. Louis, Mississippi. From there he went to the Divine Word novitiate in Techny, Illinois, one of a very few places at that time where a Black American Catholic was apt to be accepted for priesthood training.

Deciding that the life of the vows was not his vocation, he left Techny and "dared" (a word that was used much later to describe his application) to ask a Southern bishop to accept him as a candidate for the priesthood. To the amazement of many, Archbishop Rummel agreed, sent him first to St. John's Seminary, Collegeville, Minnesota (exceptional for its realization of the importance of liturgy and for its wisdom and vision in general), and then to Notre Dame Seminary in New Orleans.

Ordained in 1953, his pastoral ministry was first in Grosse Tete, Louisiana, and then in Baton Rouge. The diocese of Baton Rouge had been created shortly after his ordination, so he was a member of its presbytery. He was founding pastor of the Church of St. Paul the Apostle in that city, and, later, pastor of Immaculate Conception. His last parish included Southern University.

Contrary to what Christopher Fry says in *The Lady's Not for Burning,* what is official is *not* always incontestable. Fr. Osborn was a member of a presbytery, technically and legally; but socially and practically, he was not. Pioneering as the first Black diocesan priest ordained for service in the South, he had been prepared for a rough time. But the tension, frustration and loneliness of rejection by many of the other clergy made the burden more than his health could bear. The fact that he did not surrender his vision and kept plugging for many causes that were not yet popular did nothing to ease the burden. Bad enough to be a Black priest at the time, but to be advocating liturgical revitalization, ecumenical cooperation, social justice, concern for authentic art, Catholicism's need of the genius and gifts of Black people, church structures that would share responsibility and power — that kind of package was more than a bit too much. As Aubry said often and with saving laughter, "They just aren't ready."

Perhaps no one can say how much that suffering contributed to a series of illnesses, hospitalizations, operations which resulted in a sick leave from his diocese in 1965. The last eight years of his life were shared with and cared for by his sister, Yvonne, in Washington, D.C. In that city, he worked as much as he could, although never feeling fully recovered. He was close to the staff and operations of The Liturgical Conference, an association of which he had been an active member since his seminary days. He was one of the functioning clergy members of Nova Community, a non-territorial experimental parish in the Virginia suburbs. His Washington years were brightened by the foundation of The National Office for Black Catholics, by the gains of the civil rights movement and the dawn of a broader sharing of his realization that Black people possess in their own depths and cultural tradition a spirit and a genius and many gifts without which church and society alike are deprived. After a stroke he died in 1973.

He brought life to liturgy
Members of congregations he served in Louisiana caught the spirit of the priest in comments they volunteered to Ms. Jobert:
"He was a friend as well as a spiritual director. . ."
"He introduced us to the prayers of the Divine Office, to the liturgical movement, to more authentic forms of art and music, to apostolic movements like Grailville, Caritas and the Catholic Worker. . ."
"Through him I made the decision to change to a teaching career and to dedicate myself to service in this way. . ."
"He was a man on fire, and his influence on me changed my whole being. Aubry was a dreamer who taught me to dream. . ."
"His kind love healed the wounded heart and lifted weight from the frustrated mind and the blighted spirit. . ."
"He brought life to liturgical celebrations and he was always saying and doing that which brought joy and confidence to those who were sad and scared. . ."
"Even before choir lofts and choirs separated from the congregation were discouraged by the church, Fr. Osborn had the organ placed downstairs, and the choir sang from among the rest of the congregation. He greeted parishioners as they left the church after mass — another action that was unusual at the time. The work of local artists was commissioned to replace the commercial vesture and other objects, furnishings and decoration used in worship. . ."

The Rev. George H. Artis, S.V.D., who was to be pastor of St. Paul's in Baton Rouge at a later date, met Aubry while Artis was still in the seminary. Shortly after Artis's ordination, he was assigned to substitute at St. Paul's while Aubry was away for summer school. He describes the experience: "I immediately became aware of the great work that Aubry had been doing at St. Paul's . . . At that time it was at least a decade ahead of most parishes in both its liturgical celebrations and its general administration . . . I had been there only three weeks when the bishop asked me to come in and showed me a letter addressed to the parish transferring Aubry to another church. When I read the letter at mass on the following Sunday, many people cried aloud. . ."

"Years before the phrase 'team ministry' was coined, we had it," writes the pastor with whom Aubry had worked at Grosse Tete. "He had such compassion for people. They might be well off or poor, Black or White, prominent or unknown, gifted or plain — he was always ready to go immediately to people who needed him."

Provincial (now bishop) Joseph Francis of the Society of the Divine Word said of Aubry: "People rated highest on his list of priorities ... He wore life like a comfortable garment — simply, humbly, yet enthusiastically."

H. Suzanne Jobert became acquainted with him through correspondence while he was still in school and was a good friend all through his ministry and adult life. She describes his pilgrim's progress in this way: "Enthusiasm, hard work, phenomenal pastoral success — all in the context of tremendous suffering. He suffered from the time of his first desire to be a priest, a Black priest in a White church, and in the South; and then in being thwarted in almost every effort and work he undertook for the people and the church. Yet the characteristics of his personality somehow sustained him: his outgoingness, his sense of humor, his readiness to celebrate any occasion for festivity."

Although he was deeply hurt by them, Osborn saw through the ugliness of ecclesial structures and habits which, in fact if not in intent, oppress people. He saw through all that camouflage to the beauty of the gospel, of the church and of the Christ. Frustrations and disappointments were real, but so was the vision real. He knew that fidelity to the word of God is the deepest sanction for the pride he felt in being a Black man in this racist country and in this shamefully racist church. He didn't always feel that pride, at least to the extent he did in later years. The subtle and not so subtle monopoly that White European gifts and values enjoy in our educational system had affected him as well as all the rest of us. Our system didn't attack a pride in Blackness. It simply — and perhaps more effectively — offered no reasons, no justification, no inspiration for such a pride.

Essays like the thoughtful and moving ones that follow in this book cannot undo all the damage we have done. That damage is now part of our common experience. What they can do is continue and expand, deepen and broaden a work that Aubry and many others like him have begun — they can arouse (to a consciousness of need) a church that is radically deprived and incomplete without the fullest scope for the genius of Black culture and the gifts of Black people.

(Rev.) Robert W. Hovda
Editorial Director
The Liturgical Conference

INTRODUCTION

With lavish generosity
God has rainbowed the world
with a rich assortment of people
bearing an assortment of different gifts,
talents and experiences.

These differences allow each tribe
to add its particular melody
to the chorus of praise,
and form the prism through which
the light of Love is reflected.

True worship celebrates lived reality —
that which sustains and nurtures
which flows out of the peaks and valleys
of each human existence in its
own diversity and uniqueness.

And praise is ripe and real
when mature and free spirits in God
warm in their reality, their truth,
affirm each other,
loving each other
with the gift of difference.

At the Culture and Worship Department of the National Office for Black Catholics, we are helping to define and share the Black contribution to worship. We are concerned with the development of a liturgy that is relevant and effective in the Black community. We are concerned that the church is incomplete without the fullness of the Black spiritual heritage which has not yet been fully incarnated within it.

In consultation with the Bishops' Committee on the Liturgy and the Center for Pastoral Liturgy (Catholic University), NOBC brought together liturgists and persons representing organizations engaged in liturgical renewal in the United States for a conference on Worship and Spirituality in the Black Perspective. An ecumenical group of experts gave lecture/discussion presentations on Black culture and spirituality. These presentations appear in the pages following.

This Far by Faith is being copublished by NOBC and The Liturgical Conference, a long-time leader in the quest for liturgical dynamism and development. We see the book as the beginning of an ongoing dialogue and collaboration with all who share our concerns and hopes. We join hands and hearts and blend our prayers with yours.

Gertrude E. Morris
Director
Culture and Worship Department
The National Office for Black Catholics

THE CONTINUITY OF AFRICAN CULTURE

Henry H. Mitchell

Experiences: Africa and "roots"

The Martin Luther King, Jr. Program in Black Church Studies, which I directed at Rochester, N.Y., gathered Black ministers from many parts of this country for research and writing in traditions of Black pastoral practice. Faculty and fellows alike spent a summer in Africa — simply because one can't possibly understand what Black American religion is all about unless one looks seriously into its African roots.

Our whole purpose in taking these people to West Africa was to be sure that we understood *why* we were doing what we were doing. The persons involved were all deeply into Black culture and Black idiom — otherwise they would not have been appointed fellows in the program. We were also scholars, and one of our problems was to help ourselves to see, from a scholarly perspective, the usefulness and validity of Black-culture practices. That may seem strange, but it was necessary because very often, in our thinking, our traditional practices of Black folk religion seemed to be an interim kind of thing: done for the time being, because that was what moved people and program. The subtle implication frequently was that when we could bring our people "up" to the levels of our studies, then we would get away from some of these African patterns.

So it was extremely important for us to understand that "what we is doing, daddy, is *right!*" We had to understand *why* it was right and how long we had been doing it right, so that we wouldn't play self-destructive games with the Black church. It was also hoped that in the process we would not only find the authenticity and integrity of our tradition, but also work out ways to refine it and to share it with the world in a manner that would be redemptive.

Moving toward the subject of the continuity of African culture, I am also aware of another and more general experience. The television presentation of *Roots* has made a tremendous difference in the context and climate in which these matters are discussed. Everywhere I go in recent weeks, I find more popular interest in the subject. I would offer a word of caution: while *Roots* may be a masterpiece, it is from many points of view miserably inadequate as a representation of Black religious tradition.

One of my students starred in the presentation, playing the son, Lewis, younger brother of Tom the blacksmith, the more militant young man. So we have been with the television *Roots* from the beginning — with this student, who is also an ordained Baptist preacher, stimulating our interest. We have great respect for the effort and the art it represents. Some misconceptions, however, could derive from its popularity and from generalizations about its characters. For example, only a negligible minority of American Black people have Muslim religious root systems. They were such a small number that it would be almost impossible to discern any Islamic continuity in the American Black religious experience. (Although the spiritual "Let Us Break Bread Together" speaks of praying with one's "face to the rising sun," which could show Muslim influence on African tradition.) There is relatively little even in the Caribbean, where all sorts of manifestations of African traditional religion (almost in a raw state) can be found. That facet of *Roots* may be accurate for one family tree, but it is not at all typical and does not help to understand the continuity of African culture in American experience.

As we turn directly to the topic, I would like to define African culture and say something about what we mean when we talk about its continuity.

Then I shall speak of ways in which that continuity manifests itself in Africa today, and in the United States. Finally, I shall reflect on some of the implications of this quick purview.

Black African world view

In geographical terms, I am describing West African culture, since the Blacks who came to this country came almost exclusively from West Africa or nearby regions. In fact, all of Black Africa has much of culture and of world view that is in common, despite the differences of language, custom, tribe. You probably noticed in *Roots* how they separated persons who spoke the same language, and yet the shackled prisoners found common goals and a means of communication.

The fact is that, underneath all that variety, there is still a great commonness in the way that Africans view the world and God, in the way they worship, in the way their communities are linked together. Variations are not basic, but superficial: some groups have a seven day week, like the Bible's; some have a creation story with four days; for one group the module is 17 days. Generally speaking, the *similarities* are striking and pervasive. Therefore, when we talk about African culture, we are not talking about a huge and disparate collection of unrelated practices, but about something much more homogeneous (especially as related to religion and worship).

It must be understood, further, that all of West African and all Black African culture, for that matter, is first of all just *culture.* One cannot separate a "sacred culture" from a "secular culture." All culture is religious and all culture is secular. That 17 day module is related both to worship and to market, because market occurs every 17th day. It all goes together.

To talk of culture at all, therefore, in the West African context, is to talk of what we call "ATR": African Traditional Religion. ATR is virtually the same thing as African traditional culture, because the entire fabric of culture is saturated with what we, in Western terminology and with Western categories, think of as "sacred" or "religious." African culture is decidedly not dualistic. It has a holistic world view, which is only the tip of an iceberg of contrast between Western or Euro-American culture and African culture. We are not talking about dances or artifacts only, but about an entire way of looking at life and creation — a world view that stands in sharp contrast to the Western European world view in many, many significant ways.

Extended family

Like many so-called "primitive" cultures and religions, the African world view is based on the extended family. I suppose all cultures begin with families and tribes (which are extended families), but the African experience never "outgrew" it. People in African cultural traditions still know no other way to relate to each other than in family terms and family feelings.

Southern whites picked up names like "Auntie" for black women to avoid calling them "missus," but it should be understood that in African languages there was no word for "missus." In an African community, every woman is mother, or aunt, or grandmother, or sister, or daughter. There is no title for a person whose respect and status is in any way to be dissociated from one's own family. When masters started calling these women "Auntie," it was because everybody else called them "Auntie." There was no such word as "missus" available, since in their world there were no non-relatives.

This extended family feeling is extremely important. It moved out and it followed the people. Once a world view is formed, it settles in as a kind of primary orientation toward life, or frame of reference, and is not easily shaken or dislodged. A person may come to live among two million people instead of two hundred, but that orientation survives. In *Roots,* a White fellow they named "Old George" almost got Tom killed. Yet when he came to the door and asked for food, they fed him. They had no cultural tools for denying food to the hungry.

When I was growing up, we lived near railroad tracks. You know, "all niggers" lived near railroad tracks. It was a well known fact among those whom we used to call hobos and tramps that if you jumped off a train in a Black community you would eat. It was less certain if you found yourself in a White community. When I was pastor of a church, I saw many a "redneck" who might have spit when he left the building but who knew that, if he and his family came to my church or any other Black church, we simply couldn't send him away without feeding him.

The Black world view is radically less violent and aggressive and acquisitive than the White Western world view, and much more humane, because it looks on all people as parts of an extended family. You may remember an old man, in *Roots,* who was teaching boys how to become men and warriors. He said to them, "When you have the upper hand in battle, never surround the enemy." Do you remember that? "Leave him a way out." He went on to spell out a number of humane conditions and insights. Critics said that it was obviously romanticizing the noble savage. But the African was not a savage. He was far more humane than Europeans ever were, in general, and we should understand that. I make no apology for stating it.

I remember two incidents that occurred several years ago, both related to that particular point of cultural difference. A Black student stopped me in class one day and said, "Doctor, you've got to quit talking about those White folks so bad." Then he spoke to a fellow student who was White: "How do you feel when he says all that?" The White student answered: "I don't feel any pain." He said, "Why?" And the White answered: "Well, I agree with him." Or the White Episcopal bishop who pointed out to me: "You've got to remember that there weren't but so many caves in northern Europe, and you couldn't get all that many people into one of them. If you didn't get into a cave, you were likely to die of exposure. We were *supposed to be* more vicious and violent, or we wouldn't have survived. Maybe the land in Africa is not rich and there are flies and fevers, but at least one could go to sleep under a tree for a few hours, any time of the year, without having to worry about being frozen to death."

Now if this is an adequate explanation of the difference — and it may be — fine. In any case, we know there are basic differences between the European and the African world view. The former thinks of the earth as the enemy to be conquered. The African thinks of the world as the extension of home and family and people. Natural environment, therefore, calls for harmony among people and harmony with the earth. The Euro-American tradition has it otherwise: the earth must be conquered and exploited and acquired and bled to death, in a way that now has me living in a basin in southern California where there is enough poisonous smog in the air to kill a large population.

Had the African feeling about man's relation to nature permeated this society, the ecological crisis would be non-existent. This is a major and substantial difference between the implications of a Western European world view and an African one. And the latter's more serious respect for natural environment is matched by its respect for personhood and identity. You will remember that in *Roots,* again, a child was held up to the sky while the parent said, "Behold, the only thing greater than you are." I have not encountered those exact words before, but every African culture I have studied has a serious naming ceremony. In some ways it is parallel to christening, but in other ways it seems to be more declarative of the uniqueness of each human being and of the fact that that uniqueness ought to be held in utter awe and reverence.

A Black world view, therefore, tends to look at people and their fulfillment in a light that contrasts with the culture of mainstream America. White people read music and are criticized when they do not follow what is on the paper. A Black person who is trying to be middle class and wants to be like White folks says, "She don't know how to play what's on the paper. She play anything she feel like playing." Well, that is exactly what African art invites, because African art is done with the understanding that *everybody* is artist. Everybody fulfills himself/herself as he/she feels like being fulfilled, in whatever it is one happens to be doing. There are subtle and careful adherences to the established melody and the rules of the medium, but self-fulfilling improvisation is the rule.

The person

If you hear a black gospel rendition and a person improvising on the theme, you must understand this. *It is understood* that everybody fashions his own offering of praise to God in his own way. That is what one is supposed to do. One is supposed to know the theme well enough to use it in the fashion that befits one's spirit. You will hear folk in the congregation say, "Sing your song, child!" And when they say it, they themselves are, in a vicarious way, fulfilled. It is understood that it is *"your* song" and that Beethoven, or whoever, just sort of gave you the initial theme on which you thereafter improvised.

The cultural value I am talking about is one I feel every day where I live. Our Ecumenical Center is spread over Southern California, but I live on a seminary campus and walk there daily. White students — students for the priesthood or ministry, people who are very, very Christian — walk right by me. They don't say nothin'.

In my own world, which is an African-American cultural world, you just don't walk by anybody without making peace with his spirit. And this has always been true. When you see a fellow who can walk by somebody without speaking, you see a cat who has already been denuded of his African culture and Black upbringing and has lost the kind of immediate and involved respect for others that is inseparable from it. Wherever Kunta Kinte went, he had to show some respect for the people he encountered. *Minimally,* this means greeting people. I don't know how to walk around any campus — certainly a campus as small as mine — and do like the White folk do: walk right by you, don't say good morning or drop dead, don't say nothin'.

The same culture which affirms personhood in this way also affirms the wholeness of the person. In African tradition, one worships God with the total body. When I was with my students in West Africa we worshiped with a community. The women of the group did something which in this country would probably be called "the Funky Chicken." There it was simply a part of the service and a respected way of praising God.

I shudder when I think of the tremendous damage done by Whites who stop Blacks from dancing to the glory of God. In Africa one praises God with one's muscles and bones and nerves, the whole bundle. One doesn't simply abstract the rational part and try to operate with that alone. Again, this is a radical difference between the two cultures. So it is that a sermon in African tradition is an *experience* and not merely an idea. It is an experience of truth, to be sure, but the authentic Black preacher *don't know how* to give one of those stone-cold, dry and exclusively cerebral lectures. Any time I "gets up" to speak, I'm going to do something that involves my whole person, body and soul, and this again is something that I can't help. That's just the way I be.

The tenacity of culture

Such examples of contrast are not hard to find. I think you understand now my gist: that this discussion of African culture is not merely distant, learned, anthropological study — a bit of lore we ought to know something about. It's a vital part of any living Black worship. In the Black American world this culture is *the* culture, for there is no such thing as "secular culture" in any strict sense. That dichotomy is foreign to the reality we are discussing.

The word "continuity" hardly requires definition, but adequate illustration from our cultural perspective may shape our understanding of continuity. First of all, authentic culture anywhere is tenacious. Authentic culture cannot readily be erased. To kill a culture you must kill off all its bearers, or at least take babies away from their mothers. For the kinds of feelings and responses we are talking about are absorbed from the first experiences of the infant. A child begins to pick up the proper actions, the proper responses to various crises and stimuli, from the very, very beginning and from those close to him/her. The fact is that one's world view is in one's every action, and a parent communicates it whether consciously or unconsciously.

Authentic culture has to be understood as that tenacious. Perhaps the most effective way to destroy a culture is not repression but integration — that is, a one-way integration. As long as a group is at all singled out — even if it is singled out for the sake of repressing it — its culture will thrive. I taught for a while near the city of Rochester and at the diocesan seminary there. I remember asking why there were two Roman Catholic churches directly across the street from one another in a nearby town. Of course, you know what the problem was: one was an Italian church and the other an Irish. Both of those groups at one time had been persecuted minorities. When I was there, they were pretty much out of the woods — from a Black perspective, they had been long since out of the woods — but in their own minds they were still identifiable, cultural minorities. So they remained separate, because culture has this kind of tenacity.

The culture of work, of labor is relatively easy to change. One can arbitrarily alter the tool inventory, or the design of work, or some of the expectations and style aspects of work. African work habits have pretty much disappeared in this country. But African work organization, gang organization persists, because it is in the realm of human relationships and spirit.

Religion and food fall into a voluntary category, and so they change last of all. A great many groups celebrate their identity by the maintenance of their culture in the voluntary area. Italians continue to eat spaghetti, other pastas, all those fattening things. Mexican Americans maintain their stuff. Their frijoles and their fritos are not exactly the best nourishment, but they keep eating them. And the world's worst poison is cholesterol-laden soul food, but we keep eating it, because, among other reasons, culture is that tenacious.

The combination of Japanese oppression and the overwhelming influence of missionaries has not stopped Korean traditional culture and religion, although it has hidden it. I remember a Korean student in one of my courses on the history of Black religion. Originally I didn't understand why he wanted to take the course, but gradually it became clear that the Lord wanted him in it to become more appreciative of his own tradition. He became aware of the fact that among Koreans, despite Japan and despite all those American Presbyterians and Roman Catholics, there lies way down deep a lot of what he called the religion of the Korean shaman. So he began to feel that the shaman was not crazy, after all. And to see that there were points at which that shaman — that magic man, as he had thought of him — was more profoundly in touch with reality and with people than were the missionaries. Every culture is like this. They are all tenacious, and they all include some functional wisdom.

The depth of African continuity

So when we talk of the continuity of African culture, we are not discussing some dream, some theory, contrived because the blacks suddenly got militant. We are discussing the fruit of long and serious scholarship as well as of experience, and one is forced to ask how all that "other" scholarship that one had thought was so sound could have been for so terribly long so terribly wrong. The answer has to be that there is a certain built-in arrogance about all scholarship, including Black scholarship, that has made it possible for intelligent people to overlook, totally and completely, a very, very impressive body of evidence.

So African tradition persists despite all the obvious changes in modern Africa. John S. Mbiti, in his *African Religions and Philosophy,* says traditional religious views linger on with a strong hold and at deep levels. In his work, therefore, he generally uses the present tense of ideas and practices that are part of the tradition. He answers the challenge of the rapid changes taking place there by cautioning about the powerful force of tradition and pointing out that changes are generally on the surface, affecting the material side of life. He suggests that changes are only beginning to reach the deeper levels of thinking patterns, language content, mental images, emotions, beliefs, and responses in situations of need. Traditions and traditional concepts still form the essential background of life. On those deeper levels, in other words, things in Africa are very much as they were, despite the industrialization and the urbanization.

Mbiti asserts that a great many Christians or Muslims in Africa are steeped in traditional African religion and are virtually incapable of getting out of it even if they wish to do so. He uses the term "contact religion" to describe a situation in which a person feels no contradiction in holding a mixture of belief and practice from two or more religious traditions. As we have seen, Christianity, Islam and traditional African religions overlap at many points, so it is fairly easy for a Christian or Muslim to be quite faithful and yet incorporate in his life elements from native religious traditions. Such a one

may have a distinctive Christian or Muslim name, may wear a crucifix or a Muslim cap, but the unconscious life is deeply traditional.

I tend to resist the word "unconscious," because it often means merely intuitional rather than rational. Western European culture is so partial to the rational that it likes to lump everything else together as "*un*conscious." We are quite aware of a great deal that we do that has intuitional rather than rational roots. We are neither crazy nor unconscious, but "we just ain't following you all's abstract reason."

What Mbiti is saying is that the African's unconscious life is deeply traditional, but his waking life is oriented toward one of the world religions. He has established a link and a contact with two or more systems, and it is in the context of that contact religion that he identifies himself and his interests.

"Instant religion" is the category which shows itself mainly in moments of crisis. It also comes to the surface at key moments of life, like birth, wedding, death. Such moments call for instant prayer and instant God. Both educated persons and village dwellers in Africa may find themselves operating in this category. I have seen persons with Ph.D.'s plan weddings in which there was a Roman Catholic or Protestant ceremony at some point, more or less relevant to (and completely lost in) a full week of complete traditional African celebrations. And these latter are fraught with religious, theological, even doctrinal overtones. It is like some practitioners of transcendental meditation today, who insist that their approach is just a discipline, but who use a corpus of names and concepts that are loaded with Hindu religious thought.

The unpremeditated, the socalled unconscious, the nonrational aspects of the lives of Africans is very, very traditional. African culture is still the most popular formal religion, and its considerable influence goes far beyond those who have not embraced one of the major world religions. It is very much present in those who have embraced Christianity or Islam, because it refuses to be obliterated. It refuses to respond to the impact of business, urbanization, industry.

Indigenous, as opposed to missionary Christianity is thriving in Africa simply because its thrust is built solidly on an African cultural base. For example, in Nigeria, West Africa, in the Yoruba country, one finds what they call the "Spiritual Churches." They are very much like Pentecostal churches, in many ways, particularly because of their emphasis on possession. They are more active, more expressive in their worship than many other Christians, but they are thoroughly Christian. It is presently predicted that by the year 2000, which isn't very far away, Africa will be the center of the Christian population of the world. Not because Protestantism or Roman Catholicism will have spread that much, but because indigenous Christianity on its own will have expanded to make Africa *the* Christian continent. And Europe may again be the place that is "pagan," if you want to keep that dirty word.

Africa in America

The contrasts between African and Western European culture were transported across the sea. Wherever African people went, their culture went, and it spread most completely in religion. For the African mentality, religion permeates all things and all places. To the extent that African slaves continued to live together, their tradition survived at those deeper levels. Even though their linguistic groups were separated, wherever two or three were gathered the spirit of African culture remained alive and surfaced in many ways.

The first volume of George Rawick's *The American Slave — A Composite Autobiography* — slave stories from the slaves themselves — is called *Sundown to Sunup*. Blacks, he found, had a lot of their own life, their own culture, their own approach to things, which to all appearances was submerged during their working hours and was preserved during the hours of darkness. During the day the White man was trying to make them work themselves to death to make him rich.

But the night was more friendly. It was in those night hours that the Black church emerged as what E. Franklin Frazier called "The Invisible Institution." As Christian worship came to be carried on without White supervision, the African cult which had been suppressed, surfaced again as Christian cult. And the African appeared again — now as Christian — with all of his native splendor. The inventor of the phrase "Black power," Stokeley Carmichael, and other militants have readily admitted that the Black church was the single most impressive and effective conserver of African culture.

This is even more significant if we keep certain facts in mind. Almost none of the Africans who were brought to this country had heard of Jesus. There was no major missionary effort among Blacks until well into the 19th century. In the 1820's and 30's, the big Protestant denominations made the point that if one missionized Black people, they wouldn't be as apt to start a revolution — they'd be "all right." But about the same time Denmark Vesey, Nat Turner and a number of others made it plain that they were revolting . . . and that they were revolting in the name of Jesus, if you please.

Even before Denmark Vesey, there was a whole denomination, the African Methodist Episcopal Church, in which Black-culture Christianity had survived on its own. Long before Herskovits reached the same conclusion, W. E. B. Du Bois had said that the church was the lineal descendant of African culture, including societal ways and the extended family, as well as the lineal descendant of African cult and belief. Therefore, whatever we encounter in this country that belongs to Black culture and bears the mark of religion is to be considered seriously in terms of the continuity of African culture.

Superficially, that continuity is revealed in such acts as the dance and the walk. Like many of us, I am quite mixed in lineage, but I have discovered my own Africanness in commonplace events. When I was in Africa I saw people who had never been in America, who had never spoken a word of English. When I observed them walking and talking, I would say: "Man, I know you. I've seen you. You was on the corner under the street light!" In the American Black ghetto, where people have not been acculturated away into middle-class anonymity, the ways in which people move and talk and act are African — and very, very much so.

I talked in Ibadan, Nigeria with a young African student who had spent some time in the United States. He was something of an African nationalist and had not become a Christian, but he quite frankly admitted that when he studied in New York he went to a storefront church almost every Sunday morning. He did so simply because, although he did not understand and certainly did not agree with much of what was going on there, he felt so much at home. The movements, the whole action of the service was a healing thing for him, even though he had no Christian commitment at all.

I remember, too, a Black history professor in a Midwestern college who was militantly anti-Black-church. He had decided that, although it might have done us some good at one time, the Black church is *now* bad news — away with it. But he admitted that when he was in Africa he heard a fetish oration or sermon that sounded exactly like what he had heard as a child in a Black Baptist church in South Boston, Virginia. The style of the African fetish priest and the style of the Black Baptist preacher in southern Virginia were virtually identical, he said, but even Black loyalty and African pride were not enough to persuade him to embrace the preacher's faith once again.

The Black use of the Bible also carries with it tremendous cultural implications. Slaves were not supposed to be taught how to read — and certainly the Old Testament was hidden — but Black folks somehow managed to learn how to read and they took a selective crack at the Bible. While the White folks didn't want them to know that Moses was there, they found out, and they sang "Go down, Moses, way down in Egypt land." When their indigenous languages were suppressed and they were forced to speak English, Black people found in English a way of communicating the commonness of their religious traditions. That commonness was most evident in the oral tradition — in what we would call proverbs, or religious sayings. They found accommodation to the biblical tradition easy, not only because they were trained in Africa to plug into the tradition wherever one goes and to deal with the gods of the turf in any strange place, but also and especially because the biblical tradition was so much like their own thing, so remarkably similar to their own sayings.

They had been accustomed to an oral tradition. The Bible itself was an oral tradition at first, until the White folks started putting it on paper and engaging in bibliolatry. Actually, then, Black folk took the Bible in as an appropriated oral tradition in English. The people who thought that "they" were converting Blacks to Christianity were unaware of what the Blacks already believed. In fact, "they" converted Blacks to *English.* For the Blacks, even before their acquaintance with the Bible, had an oral tradition which, in English, sounded like they had been converted.

A course of mine at Fuller Seminary in Pasadena on African and Black American culture and world view (which examined not only Black church life but also Black street culture) convinced me that the church as institution has no monopoly on these strains of continuity with African culture. The Black person on the street is as much a descendant culturally of his African forebears as is the formal member of the Black church. Because of that cultural rootage and its deeply religious character, the street brother — the "street nigger," as we sometimes call him — is in very subtle ways at least as religious as his church member counterpart.

We asked the people in the course to go out and listen, to gather cultural samples — of the cats that hang out down by the liquor store, the dudes that stand around and talk and sometimes roll some dice on the parking lot in that far corner away from the supermarket, the guys that gather every night under the street light at a certain corner. The students mixed in, overheard, eavesdropped, and tried to take perceptive readings of what these people talked about.

There were Black evangelicals among these students — people of very stiff, rigid, fundamentalist theological backgrounds — whose idea of saving souls was to go out to these folk who were virtually "heathen" and "pagan" and to snatch everything they had out of their minds and put in Christ. But when they started to listen in these unlikely places, they had to face the fact that the culture we have been talking about was there — it was in these people and in their talk.

They discovered that these people had a whole lot of Christ in them already. Over and over again, themes of profound Christian significance emerged in the profanity of their conversations. Ultimately, the students learned to overlook the profanity or to give it the status of the language of that particular community, and to hear the real meaning — a meaning profoundly religious.

The implication is clear. Know the person and the culture you approach. If you are going to deal with these people, you had better deal with their culture, because it is there, because it is tenacious, and because, indeed, these folk are not far from the kingdom. All of this sounds strangely like an encyclical by Pope Pius XII, in which he said, "Wherever you go, graft the Christian faith." That's a very, very significant statement — because when you graft something you leave the root system intact.

THE CASE FOR A DISTINCTIVE BLACK CULTURE

Cyprian Lamar Rowe

Culture as pathology

Human beings are creatures of culture. Broadly speaking, culture is what people are. We cannot talk about human beings in the abstract. We do not exist in the abstract.

Whenever we hear someone say, "We are all human," as if it therefore is quite clear that we are all the same, we must be very careful. Humanity provides a potential. Culture actualizes the potential. I suggest that there can be no really true and helpful discussion of the sameness of human beings until there is an understanding of our cultural differences.

Earlier this week in Philadelphia I saw a television program called "Nova." That evening they were doing a kind of anthropological study of an Eskimo group in Canada. The Eskimos were hunters and their entire life as a community was built around their hunting. Their mythologies were based on hunting experience. Social relations developed out of hunting practice. All of the men of the community were accustomed to going out together to hunt seals. Women stayed in the igloos, where both they and the children were engaged in hunting-related activities: cooking, biting caribou leather to soften it, making boots.

Eventually a missionary appeared in the community and set up a trading post as a means of attracting the Eskimos. Among other articles, the post sold tobacco, guns and alcohol. Those were commodities that had never before been known or needed in that culture. But their new availability soon made them needs. The trading post became a community center and the work of the missionary prospered. With its attention naturally drawn to this progressive Eskimo community, the Canadian government arranged to have houses built to replace the igloos. This is the way a whole traditional way of life gradually disintegrated.

It was no longer necessary for the men to hunt together — a factor which had powerfully contributed to their keen sense of community. They no longer had to go out on the ice floes and wait, and then pull everything in and share what they had caught. Now they could go out in groups of two or three and in small boats and shoot their guns. They did not need each other in the same way any longer.

This broadened communication and trade with the outside world also rendered unnecessary a number of things the women had been accustomed to doing cooperatively. All of the elements of their cultural sharing were profoundly affected. And, with more traffic in and out of the community, disease was introduced.

At this point in the program, the narrator made a statement that went roughly like this: "Disease was introduced and there was a social breakdown. The Indians, the Eskimos needed help." For our purposes here, we have to try to understand the complicated psychological transference behind a statement like that. Suddenly we have an entirely new picture of that heretofore tranquil scene. The Indian has now become the pathological element in the picture, according to the narrator. Indian culture is now not just a way of life, but a pathology.

The people who brought the disease were not considered to be the pathological element. Analysis of the social breakdown did not tag as pathological the people who had brought it about. No, the pathology was attributed to that strange minority, the Eskimos. And this kind of twisting and labeling happens all the time. The same sort of transference is common in our dealings with Afro-America. When the Euro-American "Academy" affirms that "we are all the same," it is at the same time making a statement about Afro-American pathology. The bottom line assumption to the "Academy" is that, if "you" are going to be the same, I must bring "you" "up" to me.

Cultural exchange and slave trade

This habit of dominant groups of regarding minority cultures as pathological not only fails to identify the true pathology but also creates a whole body of more or less conscious assumptions which make any appreciation or understanding of another culture very, very difficult. It poisons the entire atmosphere. The pathology I want to deal with here starts at about the same time as the slave trade.

Before that slave trade there had been cultural exchange and cultural traffic between Africa and the rest of the known world. For the Greeks, the University of Alexandria was a source of medical and philosophical lore. The University of Timbuktu had an influence on medieval European learning. Going from Africa to Greece, Aesop was a part of that early cultural trading. Even with the limitations of transportation and communication at the time, the continents and their cultures were not unknown to one another.

What is more important for our discussion is the impact of the experience of the slave trade on the process of cultural exchange. Slavery then can be seen as more than an economic experience, more than a social experience — a powerful influence and a determining factor in the way that cultural groups deal with each other. The economic and social fact of forcing people into servitude and keeping them in that condition had a profound effect (as one group's oppression of another always does) on the way the oppressed group is viewed by the oppressors. Slavery, to put it bluntly, meant an entirely new view for Europeans and Americans of Africa.

A sense of guilt requires and moves an oppressor to fabricate a rationale for what the oppressor does. In his book *White Over Black,* Winthrop Jordan does an excellent job of showing how the dominant group's way of looking at the African American or the African in America was not acquired immediately or quickly, but grew up over a period of time. During that time, the dominant group arrived at the conclusion (or rationale) that only its culture was a civilized one, and the entire basis of previous cultural exchange was thereby dissolved. Only one group thought that its culture was indeed culture and civilization. Therefore, it became intellectually and emotionally incapable of dealing with other people's cultures. This is a very important point. The only way the culture of another people is considered is as a pathology.

If the oppressor were the only one affected by these subtle ways of thinking and of viewing, it wouldn't be as bad as it is. But the oppressed, too, live in the same climate and absorb its attitudes. This is the reason for looking back, searching the past, for our joy in discovering that African culture has integrity. African culture supplied those answers and ways that helped people cope with life from day to day, anywhere and everywhere. To respect that discovery does not mean that one cannot use technology, but it certainly speaks to the how of its use. It does not mean that one cannot pray to the same God, but it certainly affects the modes and manners of that prayer. It does not mean that we cannot be brothers and sisters, but it does mean that we can approach each other as sisters and brothers in a basic and fully true sense only with integrity, not in spite of differences but because of differences. We accept each other and we joy in each other' because indeed we are all different parts of one divine mosaic.

The Babylonian captivity lasted longer than Black enslavement, but no one questions the Jewishness of Jews. Why is there so much resistance to the idea of Afro-America trying to come to terms with its roots, trying to find that cultural worldview in its own background with which to filter the experience we are now living and by which to discover a more dynamic lifestyle that can carry us on? What can be the argument against that?

Talking about Africa, doing things that could be identified specifically as African — processes that we read about in *Roots* — were formerly, of course, a great liability in this country. One had to discover secret methods or develop different code systems. In all those areas where African persons had to interact with Euro-American persons on a day-to-day basis, the African person obviously had to adapt. In a working situation, it is clear that the worker must speak the language the employer wants spoken. Even the customer in a merchandising situation adapts. And so on and so on and so on. The Afro-American experience, from an economic point of view, is an American experience. It has to be.

However there were certain areas of Afro-American life that Euro-Americans were not interested in. One of those areas was the church, another was entertainment. So we find the continuity of African culture very easy to maintain and much more clearly manifested in music and art and church. Those were particular worlds in which the people were not compelled by circumstances to interact constantly with European culture.

Past and future

The overwhelming success of *Roots* proves at least that all people hunger for psychic history. Psychic history is that charting of the spiritual progress of a people — in our case, from their African homeland to the shores of these former colonies. It is not the sort of history that tells us simply that Kunta Kinte existed. It is the kind that tells us what sort of man he was, what his dreams were, what were the ends toward which he strove. It tells us that we have a past — as a people, we have a past. And, more than that, it gives us a sense of that past in a way that lifts our eyes over the mountains of our present experience (or the experience to which we have been exposed in the "Academy"), and helps us chart a future based upon the profoundly felt belief that we are indeed a chosen race and a holy people.

What is important about *Roots* is that, unlike so much of Afro-American literature, it refuses to look at Black people in terms of their powerlessness. It refuses to look at Black people in terms of their trying to achieve power by becoming Whites or substituting as Whites. That part of our past, that subtle acceptance of an "inferior" cultural position has been as damaging as slavery itself — indeed, it has been another form, a psychic form of slavery.

The Lord moves the holy writers of the Bible to pay close attention to where they come from. The Old Testament is full of genealogies. And there is an important one in the gospel according to Matthew which ends: "Jacob was the father of Joseph the husband of Mary. It was of her that Jesus who is called the Messiah was born." What is important in this is that Matthew was telling his Jewish audience that Jesus is one of us because he is family. He is indisputably Jewish. He is human, of course, but also and very importantly

Jewish.

Obvious truths can conceal very cunning, very destructive lies. So the statement, "We're all human," can be used to camouflage or sweep under the carpet real differences of culture, of identity, of gifts. It can become a lie. There is a psychic as well as an historical truth in Matthew's conviction that if Jesus is the one who is to come, he must come out of the progeny of Abraham.

To forget who we are and where we come from is to invite death to ourselves and destruction to our people. One of the most powerful moments in the television series based on *Roots* was the scene in which Kizzy explained why she could not marry Chicken George. She said, "I cannot marry him. He is not one of us. He has forgotten where he comes from and who he is."

Remember Psalm 137: "How could we sing a song of the Lord in a foreign land? If I forget you, Jerusalem, may my right hand be forgotten..."? The psalmist is saying, I must not forget, because the Lord gives us our culture as a primary witness. In making us who we are, God gives us our primary witness. If I throw this aside in the interest of some vague commonness, I am working against what God has clearly indicated I should do.

To be able to share

The writing of history is not always the friend we might wish. But we must remember people like Harriet Tubman, Frederick Douglas, Marcus Garvey. We must remember, too, that the names we read in books are the names only of those who have appeared at the top of the water and on the mountain peaks. Most of the ocean and most of the mountain lies below. It is the soldiers who win wars. So, when we talk about the distinctiveness of Black culture, we must do as Dr. Mitchell says: we must look at what the folk have done.

God works in history among all peoples, but among peoples in specific ways. Jesus never forgot that he was a Jew. When the Canaanite woman appealed to him, he said, "My mission is only to the lost sheep of the house of Israel." In response to her faith, Jesus helped her, but the point I want to make is that the woman knew Jesus as the son of David. She knew that she was different, and Jesus insisted upon his being a Jew.

God does not make mistakes. Whether we are Afro-Americans or Euro-American sisters and brothers, sharing a common humanity, God is telling us something in the very simple fact of our identity, our different identities. God is pointing the way to our holiness and our salvation by our differences as well as by our sameness.

If I do not share myself and all that I am, then I share nothing. Some people appear to think that all the discussion about and all the attempts to experience ourselves as Blacks is a negative reaction. They do not understand. They see it as fragmenting us, tearing us apart. They ask, "Why do you not talk about our similarities, rather than our differences?" But, until there is an absolute respect for our differences and a cherishing of variety in culture and in gifts, there can be no talk about similarities that is of genuine and true value.

It is in affirming what I am that I affirm God's work in all of his creation. In affirming myself as Black, as an African person, I affirm another as White. It is the ultimate democratic statement, not a fragmentation. This is the gift that we bring each other. This is the gift. The American Blacks bring an African spirituality that encompasses all of creation in the act of being one with it, of being part of it.

The power of mythology

Mythologies are not nice little stories that people tell for their amusement. Mythologies are the way that people bring explanation into their world, bring continuity and at-homeness into their world. A mythology is a belief system that manages to communicate to all the people within a given culture where they fit and who they are.

I want to try to describe one side of the mythology that the modern Euro-American world has been built upon. I am not suggesting that this was a primitive mythology. It was not. It was invented for the sake of keeping the oppressors and the oppressed happy with a certain status quo. That mythology has a great God (in Africa, we might call him the great Chief) who established an order of things in the world — an order in which Europe is at the top. All power, all rightness reside in the European, and the line between the European and God is a direct one.

Every mythology has its rituals. Rituals are the way I bring grace into my world. Especially when my world seems to lose its balance, or seems to lose touch with this God, I have resort to rituals. A positive ritual is one that causes or brings about the balance. A negative ritual is one that rejects grace, or loses balance. If I have negative rituals, I have taboos. Perhaps the most important taboo in this Euro-American mythology was the taboo of the Euro-American female. In a very real way, the woman held within her loins the continuity of the race, of the culture. So the greatest crime that could be committed was a crime against the White female. Mythologically speaking, a sin or crime is not committed by merely one person, especially when we are dealing with minority people. A crime beongs to the whole group. In Christian theology, Adam's sin is the sin of all of us. It is applied to the whole group.

In terms of this mythology, there is only one right way. God has placed Europe at the top, and from Europe flows the power (and the glory). The mythology endows the power. People who are not Euro-American cannot, therefore, be considered in terms of power. All power is gathered elsewhere. If other peoples exist, they have to do one of two things: they remain powerless, or they get power by substitution.

Euro-Americans have a very difficult time seeing Afro-American culture because, as the Afro-American shows himself or herself to the Whites, the Black is involved in the sticky process of obtaining power by substitution. I learn how to speak the language that Euro-Americans not only accept but encourage, insist upon. I do not merely wear clothes — I wear the clothes they talk about, design and sell. And I do something much more profound as well, because I try to put myself in the position of aspiring to the same mythological goals. I talk about technology as progress. I talk about family, not from my cultural perspective, but from theirs. A sociologist who deals with Afro-Americans pathologically is going to say that "the family" is a man, a woman and two children, and I am going to accept the conclusion that there is something wrong with me and mine because I didn't have a father living in the house.

Such attempts to attain power by substitution are not simply a matter of throwing away my culture. They are a process of attempting to survive in an alien culture. And I might not even know that. I might not even know it.

The experience of living for two years in Africa raised my consciousness on a number of points. I felt my spirit was at rest. I felt a peace, a secure and genuine cultural continuity. What it meant was that I was no longer substituting. I didn't have to. I was "at home." When I returned from my first trip to Ghana in 1968 and told my mother what I had seen, she would interrupt, "That's what my aunt did," "That's what my grandmother did." We both felt the reality of this continuity.

Truth in fiction

Two Ghanaan novels, about which I have written for a forthcoming issue of the *Journal of Afro-American Studies* of the University of Michigan in Flint, can be recommended as aids to an understanding of what I felt and of what many Black Americans are feeling. In one called *The Narrow Path,* a son remembers growing up under a father who was headmaster in a Ghanaan Catholic school. The son recalls his father's constant tension — trying to conform to what the headmaster of such a school was supposed to be and was supposed to do, and at the same time feeling alien from the cultural and mythological traditions on which those suppositions rested. He had to try to be and to do in ways that gave rise to profound inner conflicts.

As a result, the father was sometimes terribly cruel. For example, on one occasion when the boy was late for school his father beat him mercilessly. Most of the characters in the novel, whenever they were forced to seek real answers to concrete problems, fell back upon the mythology that was traditional and that was understood. When the mother was expecting a baby, she was in pain and having delivery troubles. Finding no help in "Christian" (European) practices, they called the traditional priest to offer sacrifice at the shrine of the ancestors that had been in their courtyard as long as anyone could remember, and the mother delivered a beautiful girl. Finding grace for one's experience, the novel says, involves a kind of necessary relation to the mythology of one's ancestral line.

The Torrent is a novel about a grammar school, which, in the British system, is secondary education, with students anywhere from 13 years of age up to 21. The headmaster in the story states emphatically that the purpose of the school is to turn bushboys from their "savage" condition into "civilized" people. So the bushboys are taught that one should not eat with one's fingers, as Ghanaans do; that one should brush one's teeth with a toothbrush, not with a chewing stick, as Ghanaans do; that one should worship God quietly and with physical restraint, not with emotional rejoicing and body movement, as Ghanaans do.

This kind of psychic and cultural imperialism can be stark and bold or it can be a very subtle process. In either case, it has devastating effects on the person whose culture is not respected and understood. Such a person loses the ability to know where truth is and even to enter into the process of arriving at truth. The whole epistemological procedure which has been part of that person's inheritance is fouled up.

What Afro-Americans are asserting, with their growing freedom to face these problems, is that they want to revive a manner of arriving at and perceiving truth that is congenial to their deep cultural traditions. What is involved in this is not a denial of what others do, but an affirmation of what the Lord has wrought in us, a different people and a people who are chosen, in the same way other peoples are chosen.

A personal saga

Perhaps my personal experience will be a helpful illustration. I was converted at the age of seven, because I saw nuns and I saw priests, and they all looked so exotic to me. I have always had a love for the exotic. So I said, "I'm going to be a Catholic." Just like that! And I became a Catholic, but in many ways I never really knew why. And then for twenty years I was bored to death in the Catholic church, thinking, of course, that it must be my fault all the while.

I joined a religious community, and nagging questions that I hadn't yet understood myself pursued me. The master of novices said, "Keep praying, keep praying!" And I tried, but eventually I left the church — never formally, but in terms of participation in the church's public worship. At the time, I blamed "hypocrisy" for my departure. I was here in Washington, at Howard University, living in the house of a religious community. I was the only Black there and most of the residents did not speak to me. If they had stopped speaking to me the second day I was there, it could have been my fault. The fact is that they never spoke to me at all.

Other things were dawning on me at the same time: the emergence of a new respect for feelings, a new attention to feelings, and the beginnings of a serious doubt about the adequacy of the rationalist bias I felt all around me. I used to go to mass, and then, after mass, to my room where I would put on a Mahalia Jackson record so that I might have a religious experience. Something deep inside was trying to make itself felt, trying to assert itself.

But at first I thought it was all those hypocritical people who were driving me out. Only later on did I realize that that wasn't the real reason — not at all. Because after a while I started going back to church again. At that time, to a Baptist church. I'd go every Sunday and I'd weep — and I felt so good. That's it, I thought. I am totally ignored in Catholic worship. Catholic worship is part of a culture that is fundamentally foreign to me. And then I discovered St. Benedict the Moor church and was a Catholic again. There I go every Sunday and cry every Sunday — and I feel good, I feel actualized.

The centrality of liturgy

One may be involved and engaged intellectually by dogma, but only a full liturgy can bind persons into a joyful spiritual family. The experience of many in recent years should convince us that when a sense of liturgical or cultural belonging is so assaulted as to lead to feelings of isolation and anger, people will leave the church in spite of dogma. The problem is not this or that "change," but the scandal of treating our family celebration, our liturgy, our culture in a casual fashion. That kind of carelessness is more than unfortunate — it is suicidal.

Catholics of African descent have suffered intensely from the sterility of liturgical rites, because they have somewhere in their bones a tradition of worship in which the sung and spoken word have been fused into celebrations of joy. Afro-Americans are therefore among the first to realize that it is a certain cultural ignorance, and even cultural imperialism, that have resulted in their almost total exclusion from worship, except as spectators.

The church, in its liturgy as well as in its religious education, must be encouraged and must encourage its members to go through the process of discovering and cherishing and sharing humanity's cultural prism — with each one of us and each group of us becoming aware and treasuring the truth that we are bits of beauty, genius, gift, from the Lord to the world.

THE BLACK RELIGIOUS EXPERIENCE IN THE UNITED STATES

William B. McClain

The gathering of the community

There is no doubt that as long as Black people have grappled with the problem of being Christian and being Black in a racist society some form of Black Christian theology has existed in America. The African, transplanted to the American shores as a slave, always saw some relationship between the God experienced in the African forest, whose sigh was heard in the African wind, and the God of Abraham, Isaac and Jacob, whom the White man talked about in America. And when the White man said one thing about his God, the African in America heard something else.

When the White preacher, as a tool of the slave master, stressed the will and the providence of God as a sanction for slavery, the African in America heard the clear call of a righteous God for justice, equality and freedom. When the White preacher preached about slaves being obedient to their masters, the Black slaves sighed, "Before I'll be a slave, I'll be buried in my grave, and go home to my Lord and be free."

Much of the Black theology that has developed is reflected, I think, in the religious tradition and worship experience of Black people. There we see the Black person's understanding of God worked out in the context of Black experience. There we see Black people groping for meaning, for relevance, for worth, for assurance, for reconciliation, for a proper response to the God who is revealed. What else but that is religion about?

It is in this context that the Black worship experience was born. At whatever point one enters the history of Black people and Black religion, the gathering of the community is discovered to be the central and pivotal reality. The gathering of the community is the fulcrum of the souls of Black folks.

The civil rights movement of the sixties was perhaps the most telling illustration of this fact. Hundreds and thousands marched to protest segregation and discrimination in the South. They were willing to face fire hoses and police dogs and cattle prods and inhumanly cruel sheriffs and police and state troopers. Children and adults alike marched in Selma and St. Augustine, in Birmingham and Montgomery, to insist on the unendurability of second-class citizenship and segregation. But always they were in the streets because they had first gathered in the church. In the gathering of the community as church they had engaged in songs of praise and protest, they had entreated the God of history to be their guide, they had heard sermons and testimonies that related the gospel to their own unjust social situation and had been challenged to do something about it, to act.

The gathering of Black folks in services of worship reveals the rich culture and ineffable beauty and creativity of the Black soul, and intimates the uniqueness of the Black religious tradition.

Songs of hope and weariness

Negro spirituals were born out of this tradition — songs that speak of life and death, suffering and sorrow, love and judgment, grace and hope, justice and mercy. They are the songs of a people weary at heart. They are the songs of an unhappy people, and yet they are the most beautiful expression of human experience born this side of the seas.

These songs are the sifting of centuries, and the music is perhaps more ancient than the words. They tell of exile and trouble, of strife and hiding. They grope toward some unseen power and sigh for rest in the end. But through all the sorrow of the sorrow songs, as William E. Burghardt Du Bois points out, there lives a hope, a faith in ultimate justice.

Created in the North, the gospel songs became the urban counterpart of the Negro spirituals of the South. A gospel song is a combination of the sheer joy of living with deep religious faith. It arose in the midst of the early exodus from the farms and the hamlets of the South. Black folks arrived in Chicago and New York and Detroit from Mississippi and Alabama and South Carolina. They came to these northern cities and found themselves in a strange land. But the simple lines of the gospel were written on their minds and hearts. They quickly got translated into songs on their lips and praises in their mouths.

There is little argument these days about the fact that these gospel songs and the gospel sound rising out of the Black religious tradition have supplied the roots for a considerable part of contemporary music — from rock symphonies to detergent commercials. Our listening expectations have been reformed by this urban creation and therefore by Black religious tradition.

Some people have argued that there is no difference between Black worship and White fundamentalist emotionalism. Those who offer this argument either have never experienced Black worship or have never attended a southern White fundamentalist meeting. Clearly, a people's faith articulation and mode of worship derive from the experience of the people involved, from the physical and psychological realities of their day-to-day existence. No one who knows anything about Black people and White fundamentalists would argue that their experiences are the same. The White experience in its critical essence is not the Black experience.

The Black contours of Christ

Let us move toward a definition of Black worship, to clarify our discussion. To be authentic, worship must be the celebration of that which is most real and which serves to sustain life. To be Christian, it is necessarily and inevitably related to the eternal God revealed in Jesus Christ. Worship is our means of transcending and deciphering our existential dilemma. It is the discovery of transcendence grounded in ontology. It is the celebration of life and the power to survive.

Styles of worship and theologies of worship are determined largely by the context in which faith is experienced. The form of this experience will vary widely, depending on what the group under discussion brings to its faith. A people's mode of worship, religious practices, beliefs, rituals, attitudes, and symbols are inevitably and inextricably bound up with the psychological and the physical realities of their daily life. This is at least part of what William James was contemplating when he wrote on the varieties of religious experience.

It seems to me quite clear that when the Christian faith flowed through the contours of the souls of Black folks, a new interpretation, a new form, a new style of worship emerged. It reflected the cultural and historical background of transplanted Africans. It moved with the rhythms of a soulful people and rolled like the sea. The Black man responded to the Christian faith in the Black man's way and not in the way of his oppressor. He shaped, fashioned, and recreated the Christian religion to meet his own peculiar needs.

Black worship is not based simply on the experience of the oppressor. That would be oppressive, and therefore bad worship. Rather, it is based on the cultural and religious experience of the oppressed. Its liturgy and its theology are derived from the cultural and religious experience of Black people struggling to appropriate the meaning of God and human life in the midst of suffering.

Worship in the Black tradition is celebration of the power to survive and to affirm life with all of its complex and contradictory realities. So the secular and the sacred, on Saturday night and Sunday morning, come together to affirm God's holiness, the unity of life, and God's lordship over all of life. In such a tradition, spontaneous responses and encouragement of improvisation are present. The worshiper is encouraged to turn himself loose into the hands of the existential here and now, where joy and travail mingle together as part of the reality of God's creation. It is in this context that Black people experience the life of faith and participate in the community of faith.

Dr. Larry Jones, formerly of Union Theological Seminary and now Dean of Howard University School of Religion, has been critical of this kind of statement, and I think he is probably somewhat right for the wrong reasons. In response to a questionnaire for the National Committee of Black Churchmen on Black theology some years ago, Dr. Jones made this observation: "It is commonplace wherever Black clergy gather to hear long dissertations on the genius of Black worship, but the documentations for the dissertations are more often than not part poetry, part exaggeration, part embroidered memory, and part personal testimony."

I do not wish to add to the long dissertations without documentation on Black worship, but I do want to look at the elements of Black worship from a Black perspective. I want to discuss ritual, music and preaching in the Black worship tradition. Before I do that, permit me to comment on Dr. Jones's statement.

prayer?

A place where there is spirit
In the first place, there is ample documentation for Black worship's genesis out of Black experience and for its peculiar genius and uniqueness. Part of that documentation is in the widespread effort on the part of many White Christians of all theological persuasions to try to add a little soul to their styles of worship, to program spontaneity, to add this or that element of Black worship experience to their liturgies.

The more dependable documentation, however, is in the souls of Black folk who disappear even from our own Black churches when worship in these churches is too much unlike the Black tradition. Often they go in search of a place where there is spirit, where there is movement, where there is the freedom to respond, and where free responses to music, ritual, preaching are not considered to be "overreaction" or the "simple religious revelry" of superstitious people.

In the second place, any serious conversation about worship (or about anything else, for that matter) that relates to our emotional experience is based partly on testimony, partly on memory, and partly on personal history. Theology as a discipline would do well to add a bit of personal history and testimony to its documentation and discourse, and put something plainly like "This is what happened to me." If theology did a bit of this, it might avoid the kind of pervasive agnosticism that is current in systematic theology.

Personal testimonies are not irrelevant. Of course it is true that as the experience fades into the distance the memory becomes more imprecise. But every book that I have ever read on worship by White thinkers was based on his or her or somebody's experience and understanding of worship in a White context. That is the context in which the author experienced the faith in the community. It is in that context that he or she has participated in worship and in theology as well. Therefore, it reflects the person's means of transcending and deciphering her or his existential dilemma. It represents what is most real and what serves to sustain life for the author.

Now what are the distinctive elements of Black worship? What documentation can be offered for claiming that there is genius in Black worship? Is James A. Joseph's description of Black worship as Sunday morning gatherings with group psychotherapy and soul music all that can be said? Is the essence of Black worship simply a dramatization or ritualization of what Joseph Washington has called Negro folk religion?

Perhaps the genius of Black worship is the same as that which made Shakespeare a literary genius or Jesus a religious genius. That is to create the new and the fresh out of the old and the stale, to lend a refulgence to the dark and the somber, to fashion a tertium quid (so distinct and different as to be called unique) out of the coming together of two diverse influences. This is not to suggest that worship in all Black churches or in all the places where Black folk have gathered has reflected that genius. Black religious gatherings, too, often have engaged in sound and fury, signifying nothing.

But when we have recognized the transcendent God in the turmoil of our existential dilemma ... when we have seen the prophetic face of divine anger undergirded by the Holy Spirit, bringing the sword in pursuit of the positive peace without which no person can experience salvation ... when we have turned ourselves loose in that presence — we have participated in a great spiritual celebration of life and have witnessed in that participation the opening up of the windows of heaven.

Ritual and culture

Ritual has a bad name among some people in our age of easy boredom. If something happens more than once, boredom threatens. Some equate ritual with a strict formality and see it as superficial, meaningless, empty, lacking in creativity, cold. Among some Blacks it is seen as the White man and the White man's creation.

I take a very different view. Ritual is a good thing, for it allows a people to make a metaphoric statement about the paradoxes of our human situation. It provides an opportunity to reach out to the feelings of others who have experienced the same thing. It allows persons to recall their own previous experience, to draw upon their own memories and the memory of the community, to express their dependency on continuity for their identity, and to share the faith of those around them. It is a way of responding to your children's question (see chapter 4 of the Book of Joshua) when they ask you what the stones mean.

Ritual is not a property created and owned by White people. Ritual and ceremony have always been important in Black life and in Black worship. One thinks of the ancient tribal rituals and ceremonies of the people of Dahomey, the Aruba of Nigeria, or of more recent grand processionals and recessionals, plumage, robes and uniforms. Ritual is a human expression and a human need. Black people do engage in ritual.

But we cannot create a ritual that is meaningful to all people at all times and in all places. To try to do so is a form of pride that cannot be afforded by anybody truly interested in authentic worship experience. If ritual is not rooted in a common culture, it is nothing. When it ceases to be relevant to the lives of the people, it is no longer useful. Genuine religious ritual has to be accessible to the unsophisticated and naive as well as the informed.

James Russell Lowell was right. New occasions do teach new duties, and time does make ancient good uncouth. Ritual must fit the time and place. I would say about ritual what Merton said about the architecture of church buildings: "Men build churches as if a church should not belong to our time. A church has to look as if it were left over from some other age. I think such an assumption is based on an implicit confession of atheism — as if God did not belong to all ages."

God belongs to all ages, and ritual in Black worship must reflect the meaning of our life in relationship to God and to what God is doing about our situation and our experience of being born Black and living as Black people in the world. Ritual in Black worship must speak to the needs of Black folk, and must reflect their problems, affirm their worth in the sight of God, and inspire them to militantly seek solutions to their problems.

Rites and ceremonies and liturgies, like theology, cannot be developed in isolation from the crucial problems of a people's survival. Ritual must affirm the liberating presence of God in human experience. The president of Gammon Theological Seminary in Atlanta, Dr. Major Jones, has written: "God is not on our side. We are on his side if we are for liberation." That ought to be the pulse and song of our liturgies and rituals.

The accent is on community

Ritual loses its effectiveness if it alienates a people from their heritage, from their society, or from their family. The author of *Afro-American Ritual Drama* points out that that tradition has purposes different from the traditional purposes of Euro-American drama. He uses the Afro-American church service as the model for his study, realizing that it is probably the most widely supported ritual drama in the Black community.

One of the purposes he delineates is the celebration and affirmation of a sense of community, a feeling of togetherness. Sometimes this is emphasized through ritual mass physical contact, such as joining hands or touching in some way. The point is that spiritual togetherness is reaffirmed and heightened by a ritual form of physical togetherness. The accent is on community rather than on the individual. The accent is on fellowship rather than on each one's uniqueness.

A second purpose, he finds, is to serve some function or practical use. The ritual drama is expected to have some future effect outside of the framework of the ritual itself. He illustrates this by using the American Black funeral ritual, in which he finds that the soul of the deceased is felt to be affected by the ritual action.

Bringing about a spiritual or emotional involvement in the event is the third purpose he charts for ritual drama. This is designed to provide a purgation of the human emotions. The church service is expected to allow one and all to be emotionally and spiritually involved.

His analysis is instructive. Ritual is meaningless if it does not take into account this cultural heritage and if it does not relate to the everyday needs and problems of Black people — emotional needs, physical needs, economic needs, social problems of daily life, etc. We are Black Christians struggling to make sense of life and suffering. <u>Song and prayer, liturgy and the whole worship experience must reflect a captive and alienated people in a strange land, a people in pursuit of liberation and freedom and health and wholeness.</u>

I suspect that ritual and liturgical developments in the Black community will mean an increasing use of some of the poetry and other works coming out of different renaissances of Black culture and being created by young Black prophets. I do not suggest that ritual and liturgical changes are a mere matter of vogue. Fads come and go, as the Black community knows so well, but there is a big difference between a relatively artificial fadism and the kind of natural evolution which is liturgical change. The former may lack reason, taste, judgment, sensitivity. In our worship we are not concerned with fads.

Ritual development and change is change for the sake of liberation, change for God's sake, change to make the rituals we use relevant to the lives of our people in their struggle to survive and to be free. So let us find new and interesting ways to praise the Lord. Some will accuse us of being entertaining in our worship, but all art has some aspect of entertainment about it. And worship in the Black tradition is art. It is drama. We need not fear that it is also entertaining. We might begin to fear when it is not. Let our rituals reflect a people in pursuit of their liberation and conscious of what God means in that struggle.

Music and song: a path through despair

Music in the Black worship tradition is as close to the faith community's assembly as breathing is to life. It has been the songs of Zion in this strange land that have kept Black folk (often) from sliding down the steep and slippery steps of death and suicide. These songs have cut a path through the wilderness of despair.

John Wesley Work, former Fisk professor who pioneered in collecting and arranging Negro spirituals, is eminently qualified to comment on them. In his book, *Folk Songs of the American Negro,* he writes: "To our fathers who came out of bondage and who are still with us, these songs are prayers, praises, and sermons. They sang them at work in their leisure moments. They crooned them to their babies in their cradles, to their wayward children. They sang them to their sick and to those wracked with pain on beds of affliction. They sang them over their dead. Blessings, warnings, benedictions, and the very heartbeats of life were all expressed to our fathers by their songs."

These songs of hope and promise have helped to bring a people through the torture chambers of the last two centuries in America. The music of the Black religious tradition has said that just being alive is good and worth celebrating, worth singing and even shouting about. That music has nourished the Black community.

It has soothed its hurts and sustained its hopes and bound its wounds. It has proclaimed that the God whom we knew in the forests of Africa, the Lord whose voice was heard in the sighing of the night wind, the God whom we met in the cotton fields of the Southland is the joy of our salvation. It is that God who makes us glad to come into the house of the Lord. The music of the Black religious tradition has enabled a people to keep on going. It has enabled us, in the words of the Negro spiritual, "to keep on tramping." It is impossible to conceive of that tradition, or to speak of it in any way that is authentic, without the songs of survival, liberation, hope and celebration.

Black music lifts the heart and head and spirit of those gathered in preparation for and in readiness to hear the gospel word of grace and liberation. This has been so from the earliest times in this country, when the Black slaves sang, "O freedom, O freedom, O freedom over me! Before I'll be a slave I'll be buried in my grave, go home to my Lord and be free," until the singing of "Go down, Moses, way down in Egypt land, to tell old Pharaoh to let my people go."

Black people were not simply singing a song. They were expressing a definite point of view. That point of view was that the God of justice and the God of Jesus is on the side of the oppressed. This was and this is the heart and the guts of Black religion in America. It must be reaffirmed in our worship experiences and it must be taught to our children. We must not neglect our past, our roots. Our children must be aware that we have come over a way that has been watered with tears, that we have sung the songs of freedom and liberation and hope even when hope unborn had died.

Some people have argued that the gospel songs (which come primarily out of the North but now are regularly heard throughout the country) are characterized by a beat, a rhythm, a set of group vibrations bordering on the secular. And some maintain the lyrics of the gospel songs are banal. The truth is that the songs deal with realities that matter most generally to poor people. When people are well off, they can write songs about individual neuroses. But poor people — in rat-infested ghetto flats in New York or Boston, or on a sharecropper's farm in Mississippi or Alabama — are concerned about staying alive. Therefore, they can sing and mean a gospel song like, "It's another day's journey and I'm glad about it."

As to whether or not the gospel songs are secular, the late Duke Ellington said some interesting things about "sacred" music at a Christmas program at Fifth Avenue Presbyterian Church in New York City in 1965: "Sacred music in all of its forms offers a universal point of meeting. What makes music sacred is not a rigid category nor a fixed pattern of taste. The sole criterion is whether or not the hearts of the musician and the listener are offered in response and devotion to God." I recognize that the Duke was not a prince of the church, but his statement seems sound to me.

Black religious tradition understands that the rational and the emotional go together. Life is emotional as well as rational. The dean emeritus of the chapel at Boston University, Howard Thurmond, has said it well: "The mind is the latest addition to man's equipment, and when you minister to him on the basis or the assumption that he is mind only, you are a fool." Authentic Black tradition is not that foolish. It erases a dichotomy between mind and body, between intellect and emotion, and ministers to the reason and emotions of the whole person. I think this is part of the gift of faith that God has given us through and in the Black experience, and I think Black religious people must offer it on the altars of the church without fear and without shame.

The telling of the story

Preaching has been and still is central in Black religious gatherings. And I am talking about all kinds of such gatherings. I am not talking about merely the mainline Protestant Black churches. I am not talking about simply the independent churches. I am talking about Black religious gatherings across the board. The proclamation of the word of God, the telling of the story is essential in the Black tradition.

And some aspects of this centrality go far beyond the religious gathering. While preaching is a product and a force of the Black faith community tradition, its mold and style, its rhetoric and form have extended into all parts of the Black community. Its style and its pattern can be heard in the speeches of Black politicians and, for that matter, in the rap of pimps. It can be heard in the streets of the ghetto and in the community meetings of Black folk. This is extremely significant in the Black community, where the spoken word, the rhetoric, the oral tradition are so vastly important.

Why is Black preaching so influential? Perhaps because it knows the language of oppression. Perhaps it is the rhetorical style of people whose daily existence is threatened by the insidious tentacles of White power, but whose affirmation of life with all of its paradoxes and all of its contradictions is strong nevertheless.

Note the Pentecost event. The main thing was not the speaking in tongues, or the fire, or the wind. The main thing was not that men and women were gathered from every nation under heaven — as international and impressive as that must have been. Pentecost reached its climax only after a man stood up to preach. It was not until Peter stood up and preached with the passion of one who had been in touch with the living Christ that things began to happen. Only then did people ask, "What shall we do?" Three thousand souls were added, according to the New Testament, according to the church, only after the word was preached.

But, if preaching fails to speak to the conditions of Black folk and if preaching offers no promise of life for Black people, then it is not the gospel at all. It is simply lifeless rhetoric. I am talking about Black preaching, not about rapping. I am not talking about unintelligible gibberish. I am not talking about sound and fury signifying nothing. I am not talking about hip anecdotes from *Playboy* magazine or comic vignettes from "Peanuts." I am not talking about sensitivity groups or about touch and feel gatherings, as helpful as those might sometimes be.

I am talking about Black preaching in which the word of God is declared with clarion sounds and impassioned hearts that have been set on fire by inspiration, by the experience of a God who calls persons to declare his word. In the Black tradition, the preacher is expected to preach — not little homilies on small subjects, not just "sermons" — but that event in history and eternity by which God entered most fully and effectively into human life. That event.

Expectations are important in all of human life. And Black preaching is expected to declare the judgment and the grace of God with passion and with preparation, with fervor and with faith, with prophetic vision, and always with a priestly heart. As important as ritual is in trying to symbolize the acts of faith and our experience with God, and as important as music is in conveying the gospel of hope and the beauty of God's holiness — these can never be, in the Black tradition, substitutes for the proclamation of the word of God, for what Paul called the foolishness of preaching, the inescapable claim made upon us.

Jesus did not neglect the blind and the lame. He did not neglect the deaf and the lepers. He did not neglect the poor and the broken-hearted, the captives and the bruised. His gospel of love and freedom was a declaration of the rule of God breaking in, like light, upon the forces that hold human beings captive.

Jesus never did separate a gospel of change of conditions in society from a gospel of change in the individual. His gospel was always and at the same time individual and social. He knew nothing of a religion that spoke to the heart and did not speak to the conditions in which people live. And the imperative is clear in Matthew 10: "As you go, preach."

Our prayers and our songs, our preaching and our whole liturgy, our symbolic and ritual action must reflect a people who, while they were in captivity, had pursued liberation, freedom, health and wholeness, and in that pursuit had found (and continue to find) a great Savior, Jesus Christ, the Emancipator. He is the Emancipator who sets us all free. And whom he makes free, as Paul says and I testify — whom he makes free is free indeed.

THE ORAL AFRICAN TRADITION VERSUS THE OCULAR WESTERN TRADITION

Clarence Jos. Rivers

The West's difficulty with celebration

It is ironic that a church which considers Pentecost its birthday should need a pentecostal movement within it, or that a church which considers the liturgy the very center of its life should have needed a liturgical movement, or that a church whose worship gave birth to the theater should need to be reminded that its worship is drama, and *as such needs to be adequately performed.*

Ironic? Yes, but not unexpected when one realizes that much of the church is virtually a prisoner of the Western cultural thrust. In fact, I would say that the single greatest obstacle standing in the way of effective, dramatic worship is Western culture itself, with its tendencies toward puritanism, discursiveness and literal-mindedness. A people obsessed with and possessed by these tendencies will find it difficult to celebrate.

They will have a bias towards detachment and will therefore be suspicious of involving emotion and enjoyment. They will readily insist that worship is not for entertainment. And since worship is not for entertainment, it makes no difference in their minds whether the cultic ministers and the congregation itself perform so poorly that they have no dramatic impact. In fact, they will frequently think that poor performance, a performance that is not entertaining, is virtuous simply because it is *poor.*

For example, several years ago I was invited to present a program in music and worship at Loyola University in New Orleans. After the Sunday mass in the campus church, an elderly lady was heard to comment as she left: "Well, it was very entertaining, but now we'll have to go somewhere to fulfill our Sunday obligation." The fact that she had enjoyed the mass had taken away, in her mind, its value. On another occasion I was invited to prepare the Sunday liturgy for the young ladies of a college in Maryland. Afterwards, when one young lady came by to say how much she enjoyed mass, the chaplain corrected her for using the word "enjoyed." When a gentleman wrote to the editor of our diocesan newspaper suggesting that an improvement in reading and preaching would get more people to mass, a reply appeared in a subsequent issue explaining that we should not go to church to be entertained; and that, if people realized what a wonderful thing mass really is, they would be willing to endure the torture of poor reading and preaching.

Even the argument frequently put forward against "traditional" choirs and "classical" choir music is that it is "entertainment." "We don't go to church to be entertained, do we?" Well, as I figure it, we must take one of two alternatives: we can go to be entertained or we can go to be bored! There are no other possibilities! A thing, a person, or an experience is either entertaining or boring. Nothing else is possible. Of course we go to church to be entertained and also to contribute to the entertainment. The members of a Christian religious assembly are there not merely as sponges to absorb; they are also there as witnesses of their faith and must therefore be active in the entertainment. And if anything is to be done away with, it is not entertainment; it is mere objective passivity and detached noninvolvement.

In traditional Black churches, even when the congregation is listening to a soloist, or the choir singing, or the deacon praying, or the preacher preaching, they are emotionally involved participants and not passive detached observers. Because of this tendency to be involved, even an overload of solo performance is not a threat to active congregational participation in the Black churches. And the idea that one might try to increase congregational participation by doing away with the choir would be an unthought of absurdity in the Black churches. Also absurd would be the notion that worship is not to entertain or to be the occasion of enjoyment.

"Going to have a good time!"

I have never heard a Black church minister exhort his congregation to turn out for some particular religious celebration when he did not promise: "We're going to have a good time!" Having a good time is so much a characteristic of the traditional Black church that the phrase "to have church" has become, in the Black community, synonymous with "to have a good time," to have an intensely moving and enjoyable experience. I remember very distinctly driving past a bar in New Orleans where a bunch of young men were "carrying on" so that someone yelled to them, "What are you doing?" And the reply came back, "We're having church!"

The average Westerner would probably consider this "good time" to be the result of a regrettable emotionalism in the Black church, and would consider the atmosphere in the European and American White churches to be the result of a more desirable "intellectual" approach. Involving emotion is somehow considered the enemy of thought and reason and understanding. Recently, in preparation for its annual convention, the Federation of Diocesan Liturgical Commissions published a booklet which distinguished between music that has "an emphasis on beat" and music that has "a melodic emphasis." The first, it said, tends to elicit "physical, impulsive, even unconscious movement," whereas the latter would tend "to elicit a feeling of response and to lead the listener inwardly into an attitude of interior reflection." Moreover, it said that "beat music" would tend to produce "a style of worship that has a horizontal, or humanistic theological dimension" while melody music would tend to produce a "style of liturgy that has a vertical or spiritually elevating theological dimension."

This is the same kind of nonsense which is liable to call music that doesn't move you "serious music," implying that music which does move you is merely frivolous and "emotional" and not very "intellectual."

A people possessed by these tendencies will more readily communicate to "enlighten the intellect" than to move the heart, and will therefore, in the context of liturgy, produce sermons, prayers and commentaries that are tediously prosaic, didactic and explanatory. On Easter Sunday they are quite likely to monotonously drone: "Easter is the greatest feast of the church," rather than to dynamically proclaim: "I have risen, and I am still with you!" Our commentaries in worship are easily the equivalent of *explaining* a joke rather than *telling* one. Some thinkers of the Western tradition, like Bernard Lonergan, tend to see mythic and poetic expressions of faith as a necessary baby's pablum for those members of the church with lesser intellectual capacity.

A people possessed by these Western tendencies will be apt to think that there is a technological solution to liturgical problems, that is, they will look for that perfect liturgical *structure.* They will always have an eye out for "new" liturgies and "experimental" rites, and they are very prone to "gimmickry." Even when they begin to see that worship, like any other drama, needs unity, coherence and emphasis, and begin to think in terms of themes, they will most likely think of themes from a discursive rather than from a poetic or dramatic point of view. They will fail to see how the prescribed readings may be linked together in a central theme, because they are looking for the same discursive idea in all three readings, instead of looking for a poetic link between them. Often, in their attempts to establish a theme, they will attempt to design a liturgy for a given day by radical surgery and transplants, i.e., they will discard the prescribed readings. This will inevitably invite a reaction from those liturgists who see no necessity for theme, for literary unity, and who, in their reaction, tend to make a virtue out of literary and dramatic incoherence and disunity. But this whole quarrel could be avoided if the parties involved would think poetically and dramatically rather than only discursively.

Another way of knowing

If the puritanism and discursiveness and literal-mindedness of Western culture are the problem, then perhaps some understanding of these tendencies will make it possible for people to begin to deal with them. To begin with, let me simply assert that *the puritan tendency has no exclusive claim to religiousness, nor has discursiveness an exclusive claim to intellectuality. Emotion is also a way of knowing and relating to the world.* Note what Leopold Sedar Senghor, the poet-philosopher president of Senegal, has to say:

"Intellect is one, in the sense that it exists to apprehend an Other — objective reality, if you wish, the nature of which has its own laws. But its modes of knowing — its 'thought forms' — vary with the psycho-physiology of each race.

"The *elan vital* of the Black African, his self-abandonment to the Other (his e-motion), is therefore animated by his reason — reason, note, that is not the reason of *seeing* of the European White, which is more a reason of set categories into which the outside world is forced. African reason is more *logos* than *ratio*. For *ratio* is compasses, square and sextant, scale and yardstick, whereas *logos,* before its tempering at the hands of Aristotle, before becoming a diamond precision cutting tool, was the living Word, the most specifically human expression of the neuro-sensorial impression.

"It does not force the object, without touching-feeling it, into the hard and fast categories of logic. The Black African *logos,* rather, in its ascent to the Verbum, removes the rust from reality to bring out its primordial color, its grain and texture, sound and odor. It permeates reality with its light rays to restore its transparency, by penetrating in its primitive humidity, its surreality, its outward appearance, to its underlying *sub*-stance. The classic European reason is *analytic* and *exploits;* the Black African reason is *intuitive* and *shares* the life of the Other" ("The Psychology of the African Negro," *Freeing the Spirit,* Vol. III, No. 3, 1974).

The origins of Euro-American puritanism are not in religion itself as we may have thought. In fact, it can be demonstrated that most traditional Western religions, if taken at their word, are sensual and incarnational and sacramental; they have formal statements against puritanical, Jansenistic, Manichaean and Victorian type heresies. The mystics of Western religion have frequently used sensual and even sexual imagery to express their outreach toward and their involvement with the divine. The visible, palpable world is affirmed as good. At least, this has been the theory in most Western religions; but in fact and in practice the heretical tendencies mentioned above still dominate most Western religions.

Sight mutes and other senses

They dominate in Western religion because they dominate the whole of

Western culture. Western religion simply reflects Western culture, and Western culture tends to be a puritan culture. In Western culture, whatever stimulates the senses pleasurably is suspect. Haven't you heard people say, "Oh, I enjoyed that so much it was a sin"? The average person has been so infected by the disease of puritanism that Madison Avenue is able to exploit our puritanism almost as much as it exploits our sexual drives. For instance, do you remember the mouthwash commercial that presumed that you believed that nothing pleasant tasting could possibly do you any good? All those other mouthwashes, it commented with disdain, were sweeter than soda pop. To be sure that a germ was killed, you had to practically gag on something! And do you remember the dog food commercial where this dog is gobbling up some kind of slop and the mother is explaining to the little boy how good it is for the dog. And the little boy replies: "Well, if it's so good for him, why does he like it so much?" Why did the little boy ask that? Because we, in this puritan ethos, teach our children that the things that are distasteful are the things that are good for you, and the things that you enjoy can't really be very good or useful. Have you ever heard a teacher say, "I'm not here to entertain; I am here to teach"? . . . just as if good teaching were bound to be a dull affair.

The origins of these heretical tendencies, as I said above, are not in religion itself. I personally came to what I think is an understanding of these tendencies when I read a book by the anthropologist, Edmund Carpenter. In his volume, *Oh, What a Blow That Phantom Gave Me!,* Carpenter talks about the senses and the different ways in which they perceive. And it was from his comments that I came to understand that Western culture is not, as it thinks, *intellectual;* it is *ocular.* Western culture is not essentially of the intellect; it is essentially of the eye. *It tends to comprehend the world through the bias of the sense of sight, a bias that arises out of a book-oriented culture, a culture in which sight dominates and mutes the other senses.*

This sight-biased cultural orientation has probably been subtly developing since the invention of reading and writing, especially after Western society began to depend on reading and writing as the chief vehicle of its culture. But it was Plato and Aristotle who gave this bias the form of philosophic truth. Plato told us that there is indeed a hierarchy of the senses, with sight at the top and touch at the bottom. Now, can't you see where that must lead? Sight — on high, lofty (therefore spiritual and ennobling) versus touch — low, on the bottom, in the basement, base (therefore debasingly, degradingly sensual).

Then along came Aristotle and, in the very first sentence of his *Metaphysics,* he paves the way not only for a plague of Savonarolas and Tanqueries and others of that ascetic ilk, but also for Descartes and a whole pestilence of rationalists and voluntarists. There, in the first sentence of the *Metaphysics,* Aristotle exhorts us: "Of all the senses, trust only the sense of sight."

Now, I ask you, if seeing is believing, what will happen to the faith that comes from hearing? But more to the point, if we trust sight but not touch where will this leave us should the truth be that some things can be known only by touch?

Let's consider the nature of the eye and its manner of knowing, of sensing. When used in isolation, it perceives a flat, continuous world without interval, without interface, without rhythm, without a third dimension. Infants born without arms and legs do not see in depth, in three dimensions. It is by the sense of touch that we perceive the third dimension, that we perceive interfaces, and intervals, and dimensional spaces between things. These latter are the causes of discontinuity, suddenness and rhythms. The eye, however, is geared to perceive the continuing line, and it fosters a perception of a world in which one thing is connected with the other, *whether in fact it is connected or not*. It abhors suddenness and discontinuity (the very thing that touch delights in). That is why we blink when some object is brought too quickly before our eyes. And this is why a people whose view of music tends to be ocular and therefore linear tend to be very unsophisticated in matters of rhythm, because rhythm is created by breaking the continuity of a musical line.

While favoring continuity, lineality and connectedness, abhoring suddenness, and being unable to perceive a third dimension, at the same time the eye focuses on only one thing at a time. It focuses on a particular and abstracts it from a total situation. From this there grows the "intellectual" (more precisely, ocular) ability to distinguish and to analyze — the ability to separate conceptually things that in reality are not separate. This mental facility comes from the fact that the Western mind tends to view the world through the bias of the eye, a sense that focuses, pinpoints, abstracts, locating each object in a physical space against two-dimensional background.

Because the eye abhors being touched and is irked by suddenness, it tends to view reality in detachment; thus when one's culture is dominated by the bias of the eye, one will automatically tend towards being a detached, uninvolved observer. It is therefore an *ocular people* who are afraid of emotional involvement, *not an intellectual people*.

For, in fact, the eye has no exclusive claim to the act of perceiving. It is a way of perceiving, merely one way of perceiving. It is not a means of complete perception. The other senses perceive also; and when not muted by the bias of the eye, they will perceive realities that are imperceptible to the eye. And they will tend to produce a cultural thrust different from the Western one.

The oral and the object-complement
Opposite to the ocular tradition of Western culture, there are the *oral* traditions of other cultures. The bible itself was produced out of and in an oral culture. But, on the other hand, much of the fundamentalist interpretation of the Bible is the result of an ocular culture that demands literal truth and history from a document whose originators had no such notions. And so to justify the Bible we send scholars to the Holy Land to dig up Noah's ark and the walls of Jericho, while our theologians make a great fuss over the clinical details of the virgin birth. The originators of the Bible, however, would have had no such concern.

A people whose tradition is oral do not have the hangup of literal-mindedness. They tend to be poetic in their use of language. Black Americans, for example, strongly influenced by the African oral tradition, tend to be poetic rather than literal in their use of language. I am convinced that one of the reasons that Representative Adam Clayton Powell was drummed out of the Congress, while Senator Dodd was allowed to finish his term in peace, was that White people did not understand Adam's rhetoric, his Black use of language. This is also the reason why, in the beginning, before the unjust actions of the boxing commission won him sympathy, Muhammed Ali's talk rubbed people the wrong way.

44

Another example: the average suburban White preacher would not dare to use unexplained classical references and allusions in his sermons or to bandy about, or, more exactly, play with the names of Barth and Bultmann in the pulpit. Yet I have heard Black preachers in Harlem and Brooklyn do just that. And they get away with it. Because their congregations are sensitive to the poetic meaning that the preacher is delivering and do not therefore need a discursive and historical knowledge of the facts being presented.

In his last talk, delivered to the garbage collectors of Memphis, Martin Luther King had no fear of talking over the heads of his hearers, because his hearers were more attuned to the poetry of what was being said than to the factual details. Dr. King intoned: "And I would see Plato, Aristotle, Socrates, Euripides and Aristophanes assemble around the Parthenon..." and his audience voiced obvious delight in hearing him play on the like-sounding syllables of the Greek names. They knew by inference that these were great men of history, but they felt no need to know that Plato was a philosopher and Aristophanes was a playwright. A people brought up in an oral culture are not only not literal-minded; their whole approach to life is different. They have a different way of knowing and relating to the surrounding world, a way that is based on the way in which the other senses perceive when not dominated and muted by the sense of sight.

I would like to quote President Senghor again at length:

"Let us consider the *e*-motion, that ec-static reaching out of the Black African, then. The subject goes *out* of the Ego to *sym-pathize* with, to identify that Ego with the Thou, to die to self to be born again in that Other. The Negro does not assimilate but is assimilated by the Other. He does not put an end to another life but fortifies his own life therewith, living a life of com-union — sym-biosis. He knows, has cognizance of — *cum-noscit* — the Other. Subject and Object meet in the dialectic of the very act of knowing; a lingering caress in the night, the intimacy of body fused with body, the act of love whence will be brought forth the fruit of mutual knowledge. *'Je veux je tu me sentes,'* said a Senegalese voter to his member of parliament to show that he wanted him to know him and be able to distinguish him from the rest. In Wolof, the word for 'to greet' is *neyu.* An old and distinguished man once told me that the word had the same root as *noyi,* 'to breathe,' so that *neyu* would mean 'to breathe unto oneself' — to feel.

"The Whites are cannibals . . ."
" 'I think, therefore I am,' said Descartes, a European par excellence. 'I am, I dance the Other, I am,' the Black African might counter. Unlike Descartes, he does not need a form word, a grammatical tool, as my teacher Ferdinand Brunot used to tell me — a conjunction — to express the reality of his being, but an object-complement. The Negro needs not to think but to *live* the Other, to dance the Other. In Black Africa, you dance because you feel. And to dance is a verb with precisely that object-complement; you never dance without dancing something or someone. Now, to dance is to uncover reality, to re-create, to fill one's being with vital force, to live a fuller life, to BE; which, after all, is the highest mode of knowing. The African mode of knowing, then, is at one and the same time an uncovering and a creation — re-creation — in both senses of that word.

"Young Negro intellectuals who have read their Marx superficially and who are still encumbered with the inferiority complex instilled into them by the colonizer, have taxed me with reducing Black African knowing to mere emotion and with denying that there were Black African reason or mental processes. But they have read me superficially, as they also superficially read the scientific socialists before me.

"Now, take the European White in his attitude toward the outside world. The White is (or was, from the time of Aristotle until the 'stupid' nineteenth century) *object intelligence.* A being characterized first and foremost by *will,* armed for the fray, a bird of prey, spectator and nothing more, his first act is to *distinguish,* to perform a separation upon the Object. He keeps it at a distance. He immobilizes it, outside time — even, were it possible, outside space. He holds it in his stare. He kills it. With the precision instrument of his intellect, he ruthlessly dissects it into its component facts.

"Scientist, but urged on by practical considerations, the European White *uses* the Other, now reduced to lifelessness, for his practical ends. He makes the Other a means to those ends; he assimilates it in a centripetal movement. He eats that Other and in doing so destroys it. 'The Whites are cannibals,' a wise old man of my country said to me once; 'they have no respect for life.' And it is this *manducatio* that they call 'humanizing nature,' or, more appropriately, 'taming nature.' The old man added (and he had seen and heard a great deal and long reflected on these things): 'But these Whites don't realize that you can't tame life, and you certainly can't tame God, the source of all life and in whom all life participates.' He concluded, 'It is life that humanizes, not being killed. I have the feeling it will all come to a bad end. In their mad urge to destroy, the Whites are going to bring trouble down on the heads of the lot of us.' Naturally, I might add, the old man spoke in a much more vivid language, which I retell inadequately.   •

"The Black African is enveloped, one might say, inside his Black skin. He lives in primordial night. In the first place he does not make the White's distinction between himself and the Object, whether it be tree or stone, man or beast, a thing in nature or a social circumstance. He does not hold it at arm's length for scrutiny. He rather becomes receptive to the impression it emanates, and, like the blind man, takes hold of it, full of life, with no attempt to hold it in a stare, without killing it. He turns it round and about in his little hands, getting to know it by the feel of it. The Black African is a child of the third day of creation, a pure sensory field. It is in his subjectivity, at the tip of his antennae, just like an insect, that he discovers the Other. Observe his action. He feels with every fiber of his being, to his very entrails, reaching out in a centrifugal movement — *e*-motion — to the Object guided by the waves emanating from that Other" (Ibid.).

Liturgiology and liturgy

The term *oral tradition* may be misleading, for generally in so-called oral cultures all the senses are involved without the dominance of the eye over the others. There is a natural tendency for interpenetration and interplay creating a concert or orchestration in which the ear sees, the eye hears, and where one both smells and tastes color, wherein all the senses, unmuted, engage in every experience. Moreover, there is no hesitance to be involved with the object perceived, since such hesitance results from the dominance of the eye whose way of knowing is in detachment.

A people whose roots are in a "literate" tradition will tend to listen *to* music. Their other senses are restrained by the tendency of the eye toward uninvolved observation and detachment. Whereas a people whose roots are in an oral tradition have no such restraints and they will inevitably tend to merge with music, to become involved with it, to dance. And if not to actually dance, then at least to give oneself over entirely to the sentiment of the song. I remember how, for instance, my aunt used to respond to my singing when I was a child. Almost always she was so much into the song that there were tears in her eyes by the second verse. She was always sensitive to the meaning of the song, even of what a child was singing as he played around the house. This was a habit that was nurtured in the traditional Black church.

In traditional Black churches, even when a congregation is listening to a solo singer or a choir, the people are so involved in the performance that they are sensitive to and react to every nuance in that performance. But in Western churches it is possible for a congregation to be singing aloud themselves and still to be singing in a detached manner — as if they were not there and the performance had no meaning.

Now which situation would you say involved more *understanding* — the former "emotional" one in the Black church, or the later "intellectual" one in the Western church? The answer is obvious, especially if you are asking about understanding that leads to liturgical celebration as opposed to the understanding that leads to a lecture in liturgiology.

The West needs to understand that the kind of understanding that leads to liturgiology is not superior to or more intellectual than the understanding that leads to liturgy. Just as the understanding that produces drama criticism is not more intellectual than the understanding that produces drama. Moreover, liturgiology will not produce liturgy, any more than drama criticism will produce plays. And the failure of Western civilization is that it has tended more and more toward producing drama criticism and less and less toward producing plays. At the 1975 meeting of the North American Academy of Liturgy, in one of the discussion groups, someone noted that at this meeting of some of the country's top liturgists (liturgiologists?), the quality of worship was poor. The response was made that we had not assembled to have good liturgy but to talk about liturgy. The attitude indicated in the response is remarkable, but is altogether typically "Western." There is no necessity to be a part of, or involved in the object of one's understanding.

Reacting in a quite opposite manner, President Senghor writes: "At a football game, even as a spectator, I participate with my whole body. When I listen to a jazz tune or to a Black African singing, I have to bridle myself (I'm a civilized man now, you see!) not to join in singing and dancing myself. I remember, for instance, Pere Jeuland, when conducting the choir in Dakar's cathedral, used to reproach us frequently for 'jazzing' the plainsong. 'When will you stop being Negroes?' he would exclaim. About that time Georges Hardy was writing: 'The most civilized Negro, even in White tie and tails, quivers to the beat of the tom-tom.' And he was right!"

Although President Senghor does in fact read and write in a manner far superior to most people who are "literate," yet his psychic roots are in a tradition that is oral, not ocular, a tradition in which it is all right for touch and taste and smell and hearing to be on an equal plane with seeing; where sight is not allowed to debase the other senses nor to mute them, but rather interplays with them. In this tradition, where the detachment-demanding eye does not dominate, it is all right to be emotionally involved.

48

Learning from each other

In this tradition, spirituality itself demands emotional, affective, dramatic, soulful performance in worship. In the African and the Afro-American tradition, the emotional is not the opposite of the spiritual. Quite the contrary, a preacher who fails to move his congregation by an affective performance "does not have the Spirit with him," and a singer who performs without feeling is said to lack "soul." As in the original biblical concept of the spiritual, the spirit or the soul is the life principle, the source of life and liveliness, of dynamism and movement, of motion and emotion. *That which is unmoved and unmoving is not spiritual: it is dead!*

Again, the Westerner would probably think of the spiritual possession phenomenon in the Black cults as a regrettable form of emotionalism. But President Senghor responds: "For emotion, under the semblance, at first, of a fall from consciousness, is quite to the contrary an accession to a higher state of knowing. It is a certain way of apprehending the world. It is the integrity of knowing, since the Subject so moved and the Object moving are united in an indissoluble synthesis, in a dance, a love dance."

I am not trying to say that Western culture is *no* good. I am definitely trying to say that it is not *all* good. I am specifically trying to say that the thrust of Western culture tends to be anti-artistic, anti-poetic, anti-mythic, anti-emotional, which is the opposite side of being pro-discursive, pro-detachment, pro-technological, and is not therefore conducive to the creation of good celebrations, particularly religious celebrations.

Further, and very importantly, when I say that Euro-American culture tends to be discursive, I do not mean to imply that all Europeans and Euro-Americans operate exclusively on the discursive level, nor conversely that Africans and Afro-Americans and other oral peoples operate only on the poetic or mythic level. The existence of poetry and music and dance in the West attest to the former, and the writings of Black historians and philosophers like Fanon and Senghor and Du Bois and Bennet and Harding attest to the discursive powers of Blacks. I am talking about the main tendencies of cultures. Moreover, the human needs of *any* people are *both poetic and discursive;* to lack either to any large degree would be a serious human defeat. Therefore it cannot be concluded from the discursive tendency of Western culture that Westerners can be humanly satisfied only by being discursive or that Africans can be satisfied only by being poetic. We can conclude, however, that Afro-Americans might learn technology from Euro-Americans, and that Euro-Americans might well turn to Africans and Afro-Americans and other oral cultures to learn the art of celebration and even the art of education.

From peoples of oral culture, the West can learn to use its mythic, poetic and dramatic faculties to construct worship and to develop a less technological theology. And this will be very necessary for Western religion, if it is not to lose its sense of transcendence. For the human psyche does not reach beyond the here and now by scientific analysis. Such would ultimately doom Western religion to relating exclusively to the status quo. Such effort would be like searching for the soul under a microscope and would, of course, be doomed to failure.

From peoples of oral culture, the West can also learn to become dramatically expressive and emotionally involved. These things, it seems to me, are at the heart of effective communication, or in theological terms are at the heart of being an effective witness of faith. Objective detachment and analytical explanations are useful, but are not the means of communicating faith.

APPLICATION OF BLACK CULTURAL CONSIDERATION TO CATHOLIC WORSHIP

James P. Lyke

"The worst thing done to us"

Our task would be much simpler if it were possible to apply the cultural thrusts with which this conference has been concerned to the liturgical life of Catholics in some kind of purely theoretical way. That has to be done, in order to better understand the gifts that Black tradition brings to Catholic worship, but on the level of pastoral ministry it always happens in the concrete. And, on that level, our task is complicated.

For a pastoral application is a matter of dealing with real people, real congregations, real life, where the work that must be done requires corrective and remedial treatment as well as an exploration of our inheritance. We have to help people uncover what they have suppressed in a thousand different ways — much of it having to do with a deep self-hatred.

I remember an incident at the Christmas crib in our church building when I first became a pastor in 1969. I was nearby and a parent approached the crib with her child. The parent looked at the figures, turned to me at once and asked angrily. "Why is Jesus black?" I explained why cultural groups represented holy persons in their own visual imagery, but she just made an ugly face. So I reminded her, as politely as I could, that Malcolm X once said that the worst thing that White people have done to us is to teach us to hate ourselves, and that she might be expressing that self-hatred.

Having cooled down a bit, I went on to suggest to her that there must be some reason for the fact that, although no other ethnic or racial group has a problem with images of the Christ done in the complexion and coloration of the people, Black Americans do have that difficulty. I asked her, "Why?" And then, at least, she opened up just a little bit. It is that kind of uncovering that is the task of the servant in the Black community.

And the complications go still further. The average place, building, physical environment used for the liturgical celebrations of a Black community is an inherited one, built by another ethnic group out of its own traditions and for its own modes of worship. For example, there are ninety Black Catholic churches in Chicago, but of those buildings, I am told, not a single one was built by and/or for Black Catholics. That is probably quite typical.

The parish of which I am pastor was formerly an Italian community. In terms of the psychic truth that Cyprian Rowe discussed, that means that my community inherited from the very beginning a structure, a physical plant, an environment that was psychologically oppressive.

The building itself is a symbol (it houses the symbolic action). There are other symbols — all of which speak to us sometimes more loudly than our words. As others have said, there must be a constant effort within the Black church to recreate and renew and reapply and redefine our worship in the light of where the people are now and what the people are struggling with now. That renewal and recreation has to appear not only in words and texts but also in the visual media and in action.

Authentic feasts and celebrations

For example, we have done something different each year for the celebration in honor of Martin Luther King, Jr. This year we chose to have selections from King's sermons and other talks read within the context of a number of famous Black spirituals. Our parish in Memphis is fortunate enough to include a lot of dramatic talent — several members of a Black actors' group called the

Beale Street Repertory Theater. We used the divine office form, *The Prayer of Christians,* from the Office of Pastors, the psalms of which are beautifully appropriate to the life of that great leader. In place of a homily, we used the reading selections and the spirituals, employing the gifts of both our actors and our choirs. As on other big Afro-American occasions, we incorporated the "Creed" by W. E. B. Du Bois, which acknowledges the ugly past, affirms the dignity of our people and inspires us to face the future boldly and with hope.

At Christmas we simply adapted a long established practice. A great many Catholic parishes are accustomed to a service of a half hour to an hour before the Christmas eucharistic liturgy begins. In that period, popular devotions are sometimes quite sentimental and touching, the children are involved, angels are fabricated, and people feel free (whereas, when they move into the liturgy proper, they typically feel somewhat restricted).

For that pre-mass celebration, we chose a cantata whose words were taken from the poetry of Langston Hughes. The cantata was sung and well-known poems written by Black people about Christmas were proclaimed, again by the Beale Street actors, and it was a very moving experience. We found a beautiful African madonna, produced in a silkscreen process by Br. Adrian, a Franciscan friar from Greenwood, Mississippi, and unveiled it during the liturgy.

These are examples of simple, easy ways — which I feel are the best ways — of communicating in Black communities a sense of pride in being. More than any words, these are the sorts of experiences which encourage and enable people to get beneath the self-hatred to a deep acceptance of self . . . and, beyond acceptance, to a pride. Once people begin to get some glimmer of understanding of our Afro-American heritage, it isn't long before they thirst for more of it.

For several years after the garbage strike and the death of Martin Luther King, Jr., Memphis was in a state of almost constant tension. The garbage strike initiated the struggle. Then the hospital strikes gave a new edge to the intense efforts for civil rights that were keeping people in the streets. And then the strikes against the Board of Education renewed that battle. We created another worship service in this context, one that began: "In his wisdom and love / God made me / black and beautiful / in his image and likeness." And we tried to celebrate the fact that what Black authors are saying is consonant with biblical teaching and with the teaching of the church.

That was news to a lot of people. It still is. Because our society is basically racist, Black authors like Eldridge Cleaver or Larone Bennett are treated by the media as outcasts — or, at best, on the fringe. That is how our authors come across in the media. Yet those same media are the ones on which we Blacks rely for our own impressions of ourselves — perhaps not consciously, but certainly subconsciously . . . and very, very effectively. So it is terribly important that we use every means at our disposal to underline that consonance between what our leaders are saying, what our intellectuals are saying, and what the Bible and the church are teaching.

The old and the new

Bennett offers an excellent opening for a discussion of this in *The Negro Mood* (Chicago: Johnson Pub. Co., 1964, p. 53): "Soul is a metaphorical evocation of Negro being as expressed in the Negro tradition. It is the feeling with which an artist invests his creation, the style with which a person lives his/her life. It is, above all, the spirit rather than the letter; a certain way of feeling, a certain way of expressing onself, a certain way of being. Soul is the Negro's antithesis (Black) to America's thesis (White), a confrontation of spirits that could and should lead to a higher synthesis of the two."

In working with Black brothers and sisters, a statement like Bennett's can be integrated in the challenge of St. Paul: "You must give up your old way of life. You must put aside your old self. . ." The old way of life is the self-hatred that has been forced upon Black people in this country and that has been structured into and become part of the very fabric of this society. It has been created and nourished by a whole series and complex of racist illusions which we have accepted in varying degrees, and which we have somehow allowed to steal into the inner recesses of our beings (where they are not easily exposed).

But once we recognize the illusions and the self-hatred, once we come to the point of accepting who we are, even in a minimal way, the spell is broken and we can face up to the gospel demand. Then we are able to give up the old way of life, which corrupts us by those illusory desires. Then we can begin to think about and do a spiritual revolution, a putting on of the new self. "In his wisdom and love, God made me black and beautiful in his image and likeness."

We are speaking in this conference specifically about liturgy, but liturgy is the center of a larger and total parish life and activity. One cannot successfully discover the vitality that African or Afro-American cultural values can bring to the liturgical life of the community without trying to reflect these values in the total life of the community and in the life of each member. Our thorough Africanization or Afro-Americanization — individual, social, parish, societal — is what counts.

Environment is a powerful factor in all this. When I came to St. Thomas in Memphis I was acutely aware that a person entering an average Black Catholic church building without prior knowledge of the neighborhood and the congregation would have no way of knowing that the liturgical space was used for Black worship. Such a person might easily conclude that it was still the place of assembly for the Italian congregation that built it.

So one of the first things we did at St. Thomas was to remake the building. We had to lower the ceiling and in doing that a good portion of the old art work was hidden. Redesigning and repainting everything, we used the color themes of liberation — red, black and green — which are national colors of some 25 African countries. Those colors, which had been used in the past by Black Americans, were revived during the civil rights struggle. In constituting the design motif of our liturgical space, they served several purposes: they communicated relations with our African heritage, with the struggles of our own people in this country, and with the traditional liturgical colors of red, for suffering and martyrdom, and green, for hope and destiny.

Little ways to a big impression
That was a start, but we needed much more than that. We needed a total renewal of parish structures, parish customs, parish ways of doing things. Given an overall vision, the only way it happens is piece by piece and bit by bit. We put together a parish handbook, principally intended to reunite two aspects of our identity that once were at least a bit uncomfortable with one another: Black and Catholic. Several years ago that was a big question: "What

are you *first* — Black or Catholic?"

The handbook tried to deal with that by proudly affirming Blackness and Catholicism together, by showing that the question is a bad one — one that really belongs with the sickness of self-hatred. And then our stationery, letterhead, began to display a quotation from Martin Luther King. The parish constitution was committed to writing, beginning with a statement on the church from St. Augustine, Black African bishop and doctor of the church. A heavy ebony crucifix from East Tanzania was hung in the vestibule of the church building, where it meets everyone who comes to worship with us. We tried to use every means that we could think of to cultivate self respect and self esteem and pride in Blackness.

For several decades the parish school has had a place of great importance in the consciousness of the congregation. This can be traced to a time when Black people in Memphis discovered that the parochial school was almost the only educational opportunity open to them. The school was then small and had perhaps 25 or 30 secondary graduates each year, but those went on to college and got degrees and came back to be Memphis leaders. The sign value of that school in the Black community is powerful.

An eighth grade class to whom I taught Afro-American history in 1971 put together a pledge of allegiance to the Afro-American flag which is still used: "I pledge allegiance to the destiny of Black people, to the red, the black and the green. I give my life and my love for my people. I promise to keep an open mind towards all peoples, to seek the goals of brotherhood, to stand up for what is right from now until Judgment Day."

In our office, parish house, convent, school, framed prints of works by Black artists hang in almost every room. When people come to St. Thomas now, they say, "This must be a Black church." That is precisely what I want them to say. Recently, we set out to develop our own filmstrips for teaching the sacraments, some with music composed by a member of the parish.

Eugene Kennedy has written what I have always believed: "The church has always been in the business of interpreting existence and it has enormous reservoirs of symbols and traditions to use in this task. Indeed, the symbolic treasury of the church — that vast, floating, unconscious reality borne of its centuries of intimacy with men and women — is its greatest pastoral strength."

That is an extremely important statement, with far-reaching implications. Symbol pulls together all the sense and other faculties of the human person. Symbol gathers intellect, will, emotions, memory, imagination. Symbol touches that part of the person that is integrating and integrative. Whatever it is in us that makes us say "I" — that is where symbol reaches and touches and communicates uniquely and with immediacy. Symbols are inexhaustible in content, points of reference for every stage in person's development.

Methods for transition

Perhaps it would be useful to discuss some of the presuppositions and methodology for this kind of consciousness-raising work and ministry. I began with the recognition that all of the people in my parish had elected to be Roman Catholics. A lot of history lay behind the choice, but all of that is beside the present point.

So I situated all renewal and its attendant changes within the Roman Catholic tradition. The fundamental rationale was: there is no conflict, no contradiction between being Black and being Catholic. Quite the contrary. One does a disservice to the church if one is in the Roman Catholic community and if one is not, at the same time, as Black as one can be. The universal church needs the gift of Blackness as it needs the gifts of other cultures.

I buttress that kind of thinking with official church teachings. And, more times than one would expect, those official church teachings are matched by aphorisms of Black experience and tradition. Worship in the Black church has always been regarded — to use words enshrined in the history of the liturgical movement — as "the primary and indispensable source of the true Christian spirit." Liturgy has been, in the most real and earthy sense, the sign and cause of our unity as a people.

Pope Paul's encyclical letter, *To the Heart of Africa,* contains a summary of principles of adaptation which has been a kind of Magna Charta to me — and which I have used shamelessly: "The language and mode of manifesting the one faith may be manifold. Hence, it may be original, suited to the tongue, the style, the characteristics, the genius and the culture of one who professes this one faith. From this point of view, a certain pluralism is not only legitimate, but desirable.

"An adaptation of the Christian life and the fields of pastoral, ritual, didactic and spiritual activities is not only possible; it is favored by the church. The liturgical renewal is a living example of this. And, in this sense, you may and you must have an African Christianity. Indeed, you possess human values and forms of culture which can rise up to perfection, such as to find in Christianity and for Christianity a true, superior fullness and prove to be capable of a richness of expression all of its own and genuinely African."

In a homily given at the time of Martin Luther King's death, Pope Paul likened the tragic event to the passion of Christ. It made celebrating King's memory in the parish, as a local saint, much easier.

I do not want to give the impression that I am interested in the pope's words only in order to use them. Part of my own honesty and quest for identity requires dealing with what it means to be a Black Roman Catholic. So I do look to leadership, not merely to justify what I already hold, but also to help me explore and understand what I should do as a Roman Catholic who is Black.

Again, Pope Paul described the method of leading in and explaining the liturgical renewal in a way I have found to be helpful in a Black parish: "This is not an easy thing to do; it is a delicate thing. It demands direct and systematic interest. It calls for your personal, patient, loving and truly pastoral care. It means changing many, many habits that are, from many points of view, respectable and dear. It means upsetting good and devout faithful, to offer them new forms of prayer that they won't understand right away. It means winning over many, many people who pray or don't pray in church (as they please) to a personal and collective expression of prayer.

"It means fostering a more active school of prayer and worship in every assembly of the faithful, introducing into it aspects, gestures, usages, formulas, sentiments that are new — what we might call a religious activism that many people are not used to. In short, it means assisting the people of God with a priestly, liturgical activism. To repeat, this is sometimes difficult and delicate, but it is also necessary, obligatory, providential, revivifying and we hope consoling" *(To the Pastors and Lenten Preachers of Rome,* March 1, 1965).

Perhaps one must have an affinity for papal language to deal with such statements, but I have no trouble with them. In fact, they have given me the encouragement and stimulation I need just to keep on keeping on.

The church as affirmation

Given the American dilemma, the church is the only thing that Black people own, the only reality even remotely capable of contesting the dehumanization structured into all of the institutions of a racist society. So the church must constantly, perseveringly, unrelentingly affirm the human dignity of Black people. The problem was well stated by Du Bois: ". . . an American, a Negro: two souls, two thoughts, two unreconciled strivings, two warring ideals in one dark body, whose dogged strength alone keeps it from being torn asunder" (*The Souls of Black Folk,* Greenwich, Ct.: Fawcett, 1961).

These are the Black folk who are coming to worship in our church buildings on Sundays. The fact that some of us are now middle class as a result of the civil rights struggles doesn't change the inner picture all that much. The tension, the hypertension is still there. Those who have gone to good-paying jobs still know that they are the last hired and the first fired, still know that (even though they make $20,000) the "man" remains above them and the decision is never really theirs.

We who are the church are a principal source of the affirmation of Black dignity. Despite all our sins, our failures, despite the way we all fall short of the gospel that we preach, we are the strongest available voice speaking to this greatest of all American Black (and White) problems.

If dignity and humanity are to be affirmed in any kind of consistent and coherent way, the indigenization of the church must take place at every level and in every area. That which is of universal character within the church must be expressed in the language, forms and culture of the people. St. Augustine said, "God speaks to his people in the way people speak to themselves."

We face no greater handicap in the work to which this conference points and pledges itself than the failure of the American church to seriously undertake the process of indigenization: of power and decision-making authority, of the clergy and leadership in general, of liturgy, of education, of catechesis and service.

At first, such an undertaking can be caricatured as "racism." Because our racism is now so ingrained and omnipresent, so subconscious and subtle, that any corrective action can be made to sound like the disease itself. One of my most discouraging experiences in the parish, early in my pastoral service, was a parent-teacher association meeting. I spoke about Afro-American identity until one parent rose and said, "I wish you would stop talking about this Black stuff and get on with the education of our children." The whole parent body applauded him and his complaint. But two people (how often it happens this way — two people) approached me afterward and broke the gloom: "Keep going on, Father, keep going on!" Today, when one enters our parochial school, one finds an Afro-American hall, Black flags about, Black art everywhere.

In liturgical adaptation, we simply try to understand the process. Sometimes, I think, liturgiologists and experts do us in pastoral ministry a disservice by over-publicizing official Vatican statements and over-dramatizing their disappointment with such statements. Our current liturgical renewal has come about, in good part, because of things that were done on the local level and in past local situations long before the constitution on the sacred liturgy was written and long before the reformed liturgical books were published.

I think we have to be comfortable with a certain inevitable and necessary tension: tension between the charism of leadership and the charism of the people; liturgically, tension between what is given us as guidelines, directives, books, and what the local church discovers in applying them. It is obviously impossible for an official Vatican agency serving hundreds of millions of people all over the world to answer the needs of every cultural and subcultural group. That is what pastoral ministry is for. In the single parish I serve, for example, we have different and identifiable subcultural groups.

So we have to be pastors. And we have to do the work — e.g., the work of adaptation. The liturgiologists who wish to talk and write on the pastoral level have to sit down and dialogue with us and let us tell them how we deal with particular problems in the concrete. I know that I am not doing everything that I would like to do in this area. And part of the reason is my own mistraining and miseducation in White systems. But I am coming along. I am making some progress. The problems are simply facts of life, and nothing to be ashamed of. We have to deal with them as best we can.

Our advantage at this point in history — an advantage that is extremely evident in this conference — is that now we can see these problems. And that is not a handicap. It is a harbinger of hope and of renascence.

REFLECTIONS FROM A THEOLOGICAL PERSPECTIVE

Edward K. Braxton

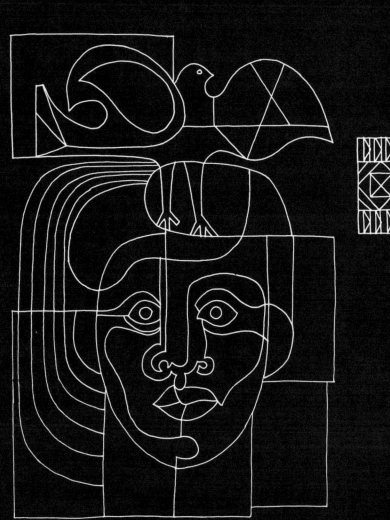

A blower of glass

I hope these theological reflections are not out of place in a gathering whose focus is clearly pastoral and practical. It is difficult for blowers of glass to be helpful to weavers of baskets.

Let us start with an example. Place an apple in a dish standing alone upon a table, and let a number of people sit in chairs around the table looking at the apple. Some may say, "My, the apple is beautiful." Think of the great works of art that Cezanne and others have produced after gazing upon an apple. Imagine what Moussorgsky, in "Pictures for an Exhibition," could do with an apple.

Cooks will come and say, "The apple can become applesauce, apple juice, apple cider, or apple pie." Scientists will talk about glucose and sugar and the capacity of the apple to become human. And the philosophers will gather around: "Yes, but while there are red apples and green apples and yellow apples, sweet apples and sour apples — is there not appleness qua appleness?" Even though there are many things that distinguish one apple from another apple, there is also appleness — so that we know an apple from a strawberry.

There are all those people sitting around, looking at the apple, talking about the apple. One could add a number of other points of view. But perhaps you feel I have covered the apple from more perspectives that you ever cared to think about.

However, I have left out the obvious case. Suppose a hungry man enters the room and sees the apple. He says, "You fools!" and takes up the apple and eats it.

Because of a tortured history, your urgent reflections reveal an understandable hunger to preserve and renew ancient ritual-making roots and to enhance the catholicity of the church's liturgical expression. You want to eat the apple!

What this conference is attempting to do is as difficult as it is important. The vast terrain of disciplines involved — anthropology, sociology, psychology, history, philosophy, aesthetics, and the sister sciences — is so complex. It is not possible for me to reflect theologically on all of them. In a certain sense, what you are attempting to do is what Paulo Freire has written about in his book, *The Pedagogy of the Oppressed* — his idea of conscientization: raising the consciousness of a people to their identity and giving them a good hold on themselves.

I have been listening closely to all of the presentations. Rather than comment on any particular address, I will share the reflections that the global experience has provoked. I will probably be quite compact when I should be more expansive. To follow the terrain, I have divided my reflections into eight sections: 1) the shift from classical to modern culture; 2) the genesis of contemporary Black theology; 3) some questions for James Cone; 4) the classic and the period piece; 5) the dynamic structure of human consciousness and method in theology; 6) the differentiation of human consciousness and the many carriers of meaning; 7) what is liturgy celebrating? and 8) some questions for ongoing collaboration.

From classical to modern

The first topic is the shift from classical to modern culture and the consequent decline in common meaning. In the last seventy-five years or more, there has been a dramatic change in human experience and human perception that can be termed a startling shift in culture. Classical culture viewed itself as universal. It was culture with a capital C. It had a normative understanding of God, man, the church, the state. Essentially, classical culture was a distillation of the achievement of ancient Greek philosophy and Western European values. For generations it held sway, and in some quarters it holds sway today, as the normative meaning of culture. In this context, man as defined as a rational animal and very specific understandings of human nature and civilization were derived from that definition.

Modern culture, however, is quite different. Modern culture does not pretend to be normative. Modern culture is much more embracing than classical culture. Modern culture takes ethnicity seriously; it is empirical, and it recognizes that all peoples have meaning systems, value schemes and, therefore, genuine culture. Modern culture is informed by historical consciousness. It is dynamic, developmental, and on the move in its perspective. It respects diversity and pluralism in a manner that classical culture never could.

Modern culture, as a consequence, tends to respect the past essentially as a springboard for the future — not as a museum piece to be preserved. Christianity and, in particular, Catholicism have been much engaged in classical culture. And in the effort to disengage what is obsolete in classical culture and to engage modernity, there has occurred a complex phenomenon which I have termed "the collapse of common meaning."

The collapse of common meaning is the collapse of community. It is the collapse of shared experiences, understandings, judgments, reflections and commitments about life. It is obvious in the collapse of basic symbols — symbols that once had the same vibrations for pope, bishops, priests, people in pews, theologians, God, Christ, church, salvation, heaven, hell, eternity, afterlife — these held, more or less and with some mutations, a common meaning. With the decline of classical culture, common meaning is fragmented and a certain kind of serenity is no more.

Modern culture, with its own view of man, accepts this confusion and realizes that the restoration of a new kind of common meaning that is open-ended and dynamic is a long and complex journey. Man, having been probed by Freud, Jung, Durkheim, Kohlberg, Piaget, Skinner and so many others, is now seen as rational, now more than rational, and now, less than rational.

Another consequence of this cultural shift is that the presuppositions of philosophy and theology, like those of all other disciplines, have undergone severe scrutiny. Former certitudes about the nature of God, man and religion are under question. Theology has taken an anthropocentric turn. Theology has become less and less God-talk, and more and more man-talk; less and less reflection about how God is God, and more and more reflection about how man is man in relationship to the transcendent.

Inevitably this has led to a heightened awareness of the differences that exist in the human condition — differences that in classical culture were seen as merely accidental; peculiarities of time and place, economic condition, color, sex. With this keener appreciation of differences, the new climate encourages enquiry about what might be the theological implications of the peculiar experiences of particular people in particular places and times. And this, in part, is the context in which contemporary Black theology was born.

Genesis of Black theology

There are basically two ways to account for the emergence of contemporary Black theology: a negative and a positive way. The former suggests that with the collapse of classical culture and a resultant pluralism, orthodox theology — once grounded in unquestioned authority of a revelation of God mediated through scriptures and tradition — began to lose sight of its own role and definition. In recent decades there has been a rash of unanswered questions about the meaning and end of religion. Some concluded that linguistic analysis and other forms of philosophy had definitively dethroned metaphysical theology as, at best, bad poetry, and at worst, meaningless.

So it has been felt by many that theology had no integrity or principles of its own. And somewhat nervously there poured forth a theology of everything and anything: a theology of hope, a theology of play, a theology of suffering, a theology of work, a theology of love, a theology of liberation, a feminist theology, and, yes, a theology of Blackness. In this negative view, these new theologies are simply social and cultural movements appropriating Christian symbols to enhance and to legitimate partisan concerns. She, who had once been queen of the sciences, having lost her sense of inner direction, had become a common prostitute.

The positive account views the whole development quite differently, and from the perspective of the sociology of knowledge. The cultural revolution has made us more and more aware of the fact that theology is a peculiar discipline, and it is in conversation with several communities. Three of these are the academy, the churches and ecclesial tradition, and the ongoing cultural and political and social context.

In conversation with the academy, theology attempts to provide a sophisticated and refined account of the meaning of the Christian tradition, in such a way that all reasonable people employing the rigorous method of the academy will be able to comprehend theology. They will comprehend it because of its own internal coherence and the sympathetic vibrations it produces with their own human experience. This might be termed fundamental theology.

In conversation with the churches, theologians reflect on the specific traditions of which they are heirs and mediators. Baptists, Mennonites, Southern Baptists, Lutherans, Quakers and Roman Catholics do this in order to rearticulate the deepest insights of their tradition and their self-understanding in the light of contemporary needs. This process is not merely a slavish repetition of the past, but a critically informed effort to communicate the genius of a living tradition. The goal is to renew one's own community, while being sensitive to the requirements of an ecumenical age and a pluralist context. This might be termed systematic theology.

There is also, however, a conversation between theology and the significant social, cultural and political movements of the day. In this effort, theology looks to its storehouse of things old and new to find items that will expand the horizons of men and women in their concrete living. This theological praxis seeks to move us from words to deeds, by disclosing the religious dimension of common human experience and the religious implication of social and cultural contexts. Hence, in confronting the scandal of the oppressed minorities in a Christian society, there develops a theology of the oppressed: a liberation theology, a Black theology.

Such a theology, because of its existential urgency, is concerned only with those resources of the church tradition which can effectively transform and heighten the consciousness of the oppressed and of the larger oppressing culture. Black theology, for example, concerns itself to a great degree with the biblical themes of exodus, liberation, election and salvation. This last form of theology might be termed applied or practical theology.

The second, positive account of how contemporary Black theology appeared on the scene is, I believe, both more helpful and more correct. Black theology is a relatively new phenomenon on the American theological scene — at least, as a formal corpus. Yet its origins are as ancient as the rich religious culture of Africa (outlined so eloquently in this conference) and its roots are found in the free and post Civil War experiences of slaves. It found beautiful expression in spirituals, sermons, blues, and stories of an oppressed people. Its contemporary spokesmen are a group of creative Protestant scholars who, as D. Otis Roberts declared, "are not restrained by Catholic dogma."

While Martin Luther King, Jr. might be the admired patriarch of the present generation of Black theologians, his tempered views are not dominant in the writings of those on the scene today. In summary, they and their central themes are: a) Joseph Washington — the oppressed Blacks are God's chosen people; b) Albert Cleage, Jr. — Jesus is, indeed, the Black messiah; c) J. D. Otis Roberts — there is a compatibility and reconciliation with the thrust of Black liberation theology in a universal Christian vision; d) Eulalio Balthasar — White, Western theology sustains racism by supporting a color symbolism that sees white as good and black as evil; e) Major Jones — enriching Black liberation theology by constructing a Christian ethics of freedom based on agape; f) William Jones — the problem of evil framed in the compelling question, "Is God a White racist?"; g) Cecil W. Cohn — an identity crisis in Black theology due to neglect of the experience of an almighty sovereign God as the point of departure for all Black theology; and finally, h) James H. Cone, whose central theme is the joining of Black power with the biblical depiction of the God of the Exodus and the New Testament Jesus, who proclaims good news to the poor, release to captives, for the construction of a radical Black theology of liberation.

Questions for James Cone

James Cone's work is probably the most systematic and he has produced the largest corpus. Time will not permit even a resume. In his works, however, Cone has indicated a number of questions and suggested a number of attitudes that relate to the program of this conference. He insists that there are certain questions that emerge in classical Western, White theology, which he considers not to be on the Black agenda. Such questions as rational arguments for the existence or non-existence of God, the christological questions of the early councils, metaphysical explanations for the problem of evil, questions about the cognitive content of biblical texts, the relationship of the assertions of religion to the advances of science — these are White questions, in Cone's view, while Black questions are those necessary for the existential survival of a people, for their liberation, their uplifting, their transformation.

I believe that this dichotomy, to the degree that I have heard it correctly in James Cone, and to the degree that I think I have heard it occasionally in this conference, is unfortunate. The question that must be asked is this: For which Blacks are these non-questions? Obviously, those involved in the immediate struggle for survival, in past or present, are not likely to entertain metaphysical speculations any more than one who is starving is likely to discuss the nature of appleness. Nor are these questions for White people whose material existence is threatened. Mention was made yesterday of the people in Appalachia. I suspect that the hill folk of Tennessee would not sit about discussing any of these questions, even though they are certainly White.

These are questions, I suggest, which in different formulations may be questions for some Black Christians in the pews, some Black college students, some Black ministers, and some Black scholars. For a liberal theology, which James Cone and his colleagues have proposed, his work seems to me to be marred by a strange kind of dogmatism. The dogmatism is reflected in what I find as his and others' inability to answer what is for me a controlling question: What constitutes an authentic Black experience? What constitutes the accrediting agency for genuine Blackness? Who gives the stamp of approval, if you will, to someone's postures, attitudes, points of view, as being genuinely Black?

That is a very difficult question to answer. So far, I have not heard a satisfactory reply. In reading some of the literature, which I respect and consider most significant, I get the distinct impression that unless one's priorities are dominated by the desire to overcome racial injustice in America, unless one's aesthetics and intellectual concerns follow and flow in certain paths, unless one's cultural preferences are of a certain type, one does not truly participate in the Black experience.

But I think it can be argued that it is an empirical fact that the Black experience in the United States is a complex, multi-faceted and multi-dimensional reality. It may be rural, urban, or suburban. It may be lower class, middle, or upper. It may be Baptist, Presbyterian, Methodist, Lutheran, or Catholic. It may be devout or irreligious. It may be politically conservative or activist. There are Black families who prefer to think of themselves as Negroes or people of color and not as Blacks. My experience indicates that many Black Catholics are of a more conservative style, frequently preferring the "Pange Lingua" to the "Missa Luba" *(why* this is the case and whether or not this is good is a further question). It would seem to me that the experiences of some of the writers I have mentioned so significantly influence their horizons that those particular experiences become almost normative for an authentic Black experience.

Much as one may applaud Alex Haley's brilliant achievement in *Roots,* it remains a fact that in most cases the contemporary Black American is a peculiar hybrid of both African and European cultures. While a good case — and an urgent case — must be made that the one must be reappropriated, by what necessity do we argue that the other must be cast off, and by what process is this done?

We were fortunate to have Alex Haley as a guest of Harvard University this Fall and I had the opportunity to speak with him about his twelve years' search. I put this question of "mixed roots" to him. He said that when he stood among his cousins in the Gambia there was a love-hate feeling present. On the one hand, it was his family and he wanted to cut himself off from his past context and live there. On the other hand, he was a foreigner, a stranger from Beverly Hills, California, in a strange land. He realized that he was a person who could not change the clock of history: he had one foot in one world, one in another, and that was peculiarly his identity, which he must develop, refine, grasp and appropriate.

To the degree that the question of what is an authentic Black experience is not answered, there is a great danger that a kind of self-stereotyping will occur on the part of a people. Fastening on certain styles, idioms, modes of thinking, attitudes, and affects, while blinding one's eyes to other aspects of one's experience, can result in a narrow self-definition. And this latter will not be too much different, in a certain sense, from a previous White stereotypical view of Blacks and their soulful worship, natural musical rhythm, informal style of gathering, concrete rather than abstract modes of thought, and so on. We may unwittingly be guilty of re-stereotyping ourselves if we are satisfied with too narrow a definition of what constitutes a Black experience.

To deny a place on the Black agenda for speculative metaphysical questions is to suggest that Black theologians be excluded from the conversations mentioned above, involving fundamental and systematic theology, and be confined to the area of practical theology alone, simply because of its contemporary exigencies.

I believe that a refinement of the problem can be achieved by a distinction which I hope is clear in my brief statement of it. That is the distinction between two worlds. We all live in many worlds, of course, but two worlds I have in mind are the world of common sense and the world of theory. The world of common sense — the one that preoccupies most of us most of the time — deals with our personal needs, our desires, our expectations. The world of common sense is the intersubjective world of personal meaning. It is descriptive, evocative and self-involving in a very special way. From the perspective of the world of common sense, we say, "The sun rises and the sun sets." But the raising and the answering of a further relevant question can nudge an individual from the world of common sense into the world of theory.

The world of theory seeks explanations, not descriptions. It relates realities to one another, not to an individual. In the world of common sense, one may experience a feeling of unshakable conviction that one has been touched by God. But this does not mean that the same person may not subsequently raise questions concerning the condition of the possibility of such an experience. Was the experience simply an experience of their interiority, or can rational arguments be adduced to ground the validity of such experience? In the world of theory we may say that while it appears that the sun rises and sets, in fact, the earth moves in an elliptical circle about the sun.

To be sure, Cone and others are unquestionably correct in arguing the importance of social context and the fact that any theology — even the great Western theology, the German theologians who have dominated American theology for so long — is always colored by a perspective. This is a necessary and critical caution for anyone who is inclined to assert that his or her theological statements are universal.

However, to dichotomize speculative and pragmatic theology, the world of theory from the world of common sense — in the way that I suspect it is sometimes being done — is, to me methodologically unacceptable. It suggests that, because of some kind of socio-cultural context or racial disposition, some can do one and not the other. I believe it is possible to live in both worlds: to know that from the point of view of common sense, the sun rises

66

and sets, and to know also that from the point of view of theory, the earth moves in an elliptical circle around the sun. While there may be a compelling urgency for an existential practical theology in the Black community, this should not lead to the rejection of critical speculative thought.

The classic and the period piece

I must be very brief at this point, but the nature of the classic and the period piece is something I have been thinking about as a result of conversations with David Tracy. The idea comes from literary criticism but it has implications for theology, and religious experience, and, in the context of this colloquium, for liturgy.

Black Catholic liturgy is something new on the horizon — an attempt to enflesh the celebrations of common prayer with indigenous elements peculiar to the worshiping community. It is a very good thing for the American church. Ethnocentric liturgy is not new. All the liturgy that we have ever had was ethnocentric. It was simply someone else's ethnicity that was being mediated. Ethnocentric liturgy need not be a retreat to particularism or negative forms of nationalism or a privatized form of navel gazing. As a matter of fact, the denial of the negative connotations of the melting-pot American paradigm and the retrieval of ethnicity may signal the possibility of future theological and liturgical classics.

A "classic" is not necessarily something from the classical period. A "classic" is a piece of literature, art, poetry — any of the creations of the human spirit — that is so extraordinary, usually in its penetration of the particular, that it illuminates the human spirit in such a way that any attentive person can be transformed by the experience. By penetrating a classic, one enters into the world that it opens.

A period piece, on the other hand, may be something quite excellent or quite interesting, quite significant at a particular matrix in history, quite helpful for people in a particular context and time, but it is always something that is dated. If it is later studied, it is studied only because it was interesting in its own particular context and is there illustrative of a period.

The christological statements of Chalcedon, for example, are theological classics — not because the nature of persons, substance, distinctions are eternal, but because the profoundness of the penetration can illuminate the mystery of Jesus for anyone who takes the time to study them. On the other hand, the detailed discussions of certain theologians about the biological condition of the womb of Mary at the time of Jesus' birth are at best a period piece.

It is evident that great classics in our secular as well as our religious traditions are at once deeply personal and particular in their origins and expression, while being at the same time public and universal in their power to transform the human spirit. Cyprian Rowe made the statement that in affirming himself as Black, he affirms someone else as White. In penetrating our own identity, our own interiority, we also provide the condition of the possibility of entering someone else's world. In making a classic disclosing statement about ourselves, we recognize the classic possibility of another's disclosure.

Paradoxically, the profound penetration of a specific cultural, social, or religious heritage may result in an expression that is universal in its power to illuminate the human spirit. Louis Armstrong and Billie Holliday produced very particularized musical forms in American jazz and blues. Yet their works are acclaimed as classics in the same manner that the symphonies of Beethoven are classics, because they have the singular capacity to touch and transform the spirit of any attentive listener.

In our culture we have a great need to experience the classic in every context: secular and liturgical. Otherwise, we will have a generation of people who know nothing of Melville's *Moby Dick,* the *classic* story of the menacing and seductive presence of evil that can be symbolized by the sea and the sea beasts. We will have a generation that thinks Peter Benchley's *Jaws* is the best sea story ever. We do have people who think that Segal's *Love Story* is a classic, when it is, at best, a period piece, but who do not even know *Romeo and Juliet,* the classic statement of tragedy in romantic love.

Remarkably — and this is important — one need not have had the experience in order to be touched and transformed by the illuminating insights presented in a classic, *if* one has an attentive spirit (a big if). One need not be a member of a problem-laden Irish-American family in order to be stunned and challenged by an experience of Eugene O'Neill's *Long Day's Journey into Night,* nor need one have personal experience of the special pains and tragedies of Black urban tenement dwellers in order to participate fully in the catharsis of Lorraine Hansberry's classic play, *A Raisin in the Sun.* These examples are in stark contrast to the vulgar, exploitative sensationalism found in such works as *All in the Family* or *Superfly,* which, in my judgment, are not even period pieces.

The same can be said of liturgical expression. Gregorian chant is not significant because it is holy. It is not holy — it is just music, but it is a classic expression. Someone mentioned "Amazing Grace" and the fact that it was written by a slaver. I think it can be argued that both Gregorian chant and "Amazing Grace" will remain within the religious consciousness of people as significant expressions, because of their classic possibility as aesthetic statements, depending on an individual's and a community's state of culture, disposition and attentiveness.

Christianity in general and Catholicism in particular would be much enhanced if the American Black Catholic context could produce a classic instance of worship, rather than a period piece. I have no doubt whatever that the rich elements that make up the Black Catholic experience contain the potential for such a classic, but patience, trust and freedom must abound if it is to come about. As far as I am concerned, anything becomes a period piece if it consists of patched together bits and bandaids from various other worship contexts or experiences which have never been interiorized, personally appropriated by the worshiping congregation. There most certainly can be a reclaiming and reappropriating of submerged (or even rejected) identity, but that must be happening interiorly before its artistic expression can become a classic.

Dynamic structure of human consciousness

Many of the things that have been said during these reflections deal with the human person, the human condition, the human subject. It might be helpful to sort out what I have concluded to be one of the best explanations (or best schemes) of the structure of the total person, at least in his or her interiority. Bernard Lonergan has suggested that human consciousness is a self-assembling structure on four levels: experience, understanding, judgment and commitment.

The level of experience is the empirical level. This first level confronts the world as a whole. Here are all the data of our inner and outer world of experience and, to a certain degree, consciousness is undifferentiated. The second is the level of intellectual understanding. It is called forth automatically by experience, for when we encounter anything we say, at some point and to some degree, "Well, what is it?" Hypotheses are put forth; there is enquiry and formulation.

This activates the rational level, the level of judgment. Now we weigh and marshal evidence. The question of truth occurs, and we ask, "Is it so? Is that the case?" This level has to do with the concern for objectivity. On the fourth level of human consciousness, again called forth by the previous one, there occurs further penetration: "Is it valuable? Is is worthwhile?" This is the level of commitment, the responsible level. This moves us from words to deeds and it involves the whole person. Affect-laden images, symbols and mythopoeic meaning systems emerge on this level.

There is a certain sense in which truth is operative on both the third and the fourth levels. On the third, the question is more objective and more detached — what Lonergan calls the result of pure, disinterested, unrestricted desire to know. On the fourth, there is self-involvement — the affectivity, the feelings and the visceral involvement of the total person.

It is possible, from this structure of human consciouness, to extrapolate a scheme for accounting for what theologians have done in the past and, more helpfully, an argument for what they should be doing in the present and in the future, if we hope to have ongoing collaboration. That scheme suggests that the four levels of human consciousness can be related to both the past tradition and the present situation of the church, resulting in producing eight functional specializations, or eight particular activities in the theological enterprise.

These eight activities are: a) Research (related to experience above) — what happened, what are the data, the charter documents, the New Testament text, the liturgical texts, everything about that previous context? b) Interpretation (related to understanding) — what do the documents and artifacts and particular things brought together mean, and, more importantly, what did they mean in the context in which they emerged, and what could they mean in the context in which they are going to be appropriated?

c) History (related to judgment) — the meanings and contexts of the past are diverse and they have a history which is sometimes onward movement and sometimes a dead end. d) Dialectics (related to commitment) — when one begins to enquire about any theological subject, one finds that this procedure leaves one with a plurality of possible conclusions. Dialectic results in a process called position and counter-position. Positions that are valid over time — perhaps centuries — will invite development, those which are invalid (i.e., counter-positions) invite reversal and decline. This is because of the affirmation of a certain self-correcting process in human learning.

e) Foundation — to move from dialectics to foundation, out of a plurality of fundamental propositions or fundamental insights or experiences, conversion must occur. Conversion, as Lonergan has described it, is the transformation of one's horizon, one's interiority, by which one sees the world from a completely different prospective. Conversion may be religious; it may be theistic; it may be Christian; it may be ecclesial; it may be intellectual; it may be moral. Ideally, it is all of these. It is religious when one shifts from looking at the world as so much "sound and fury, signifying nothing," to a gaze that apprehends the world as ultimately meaningful. This involves awareness of what Rudolph Otto calls "the holy."

Religious conversion becomes theistic when ultimacy is focused in a personal, gracious ground of reality, in Paul Tillich's terms. It becomes Christian when this gracious love and reality is paradigmatically disclosed in the life and ministry of Jesus of Nazareth, exalted as the Christ. It becomes ecclesial when this commitment to Jesus, exalted as the Christ, is celebrated in community with others, with a past tradition, a present context, and a future hope. It becomes moral when the affirmations of the earlier conversions move one from words to deeds, and one recognizes that there is an intrinsic relationship between one's religious horizon and one's concrete life style. So, one acts not because of pleasure, not because of satisfaction, but because of values. Here I am not using the word "pleasure" in the positive sense (described elsewhere in this conference) of the interior, and involving the communal, entertaining and joyful experience of liturgy, but pleasure with the negative connotations of hedonistic egocentricity. Intellectual conversion is disciplined human inquiry marked by a humble recognition of the limits of language, the historicity of the person and the permanence of mystery.

Conversion is the only way to make this move. Sometimes in the past that was not what was argued in Catholic theology. It was argued that simply by doing your homework and studying the scriptures and the documents, one could prove that Peter was the first pope and that every pope since Peter has a link with the first pope. But if we acknowledge that the Lutherans, the Methodists, the Anglicans, and everybody else can also do their homework, why is it that only Catholics can get to this foundation simply by that application?

No, the way is by conversion. Once conversion occurs, however, one can move on to the fifth functional specialty, foundations. An example of foundation would be an affirmation on the part of a people that Jesus is the Lord, Jesus is the Christ, Jesus is the paradigmatic figure of God's love. That may be all that is necessary. This provides faith in the broad sense, the context and horizon for subsequent beliefs.

These foundations become more specific in f) Doctrines — doctrines which spell that broad faith out in a belief system. What does it mean to say that Jesus is Lord? Well, Jesus is the Son of God, he's the Christ, the Messiah, the Redeemer. All of the rest is spelled out in doctrines. And then that leads to the next functional specialty: g) Systematics — how can we talk about this in a coherent language that makes sense to us and to other people, and to people outside of our context. So we get philosophical language. We get the great councils of Nicaea and Chalcedon, apologists like Justin Martyr and Ignatius of Antioch. In the contemporary context, we have theologians in the academy, in the socio-cultural context, and in the ecclesial tradition. All contributing to the formulation of a systematic statement.

And finally, most relevant to our discussion, the functional specialty: h) Communication. Communication is the activity in which liturgy, catechesis, preaching and all the rest take their final form. But what are they mediating? What is it they are communicating? Are they communicating something from this kind of a process? They may be and they may not be. Communication is the context where one discerns whether, for this people in this situation and in this place, this or that medium (music, art, ceremony, ritual, image, etc.) is helpful and effective. There must be a discernment of, among other things, appropriateness in the here and now — sermon? lecture? multi-media presentation? cathechesis? pre-evangelization? short talk? movie? piece of music? sharing? serendipity? The communicator bears a great responsibility. He is an artist: the parish priest, the pastoral team discerning and transforming the present with memory of the past and with vision of the future.

One of the reasons why communication is so difficult is the fact that the human subject is so complex. Liturgy and worship engage the whole person with his/her complex history. Human consciousness flows in many forms and patterns. It is polymorphic and usually undifferentiated. That is, the various worlds in which we live are never sorted out, thought out, personally appropriated, so that we do not recognize that we move now from the world of immediacy to the world mediated by meaning, now from the world of common sense to the world of theory. When we are unaware of these differences, there is, eventually, cognitive disharmony.

Differentiation of consciousness

What do I mean? The world of immediacy is the world of the infant in his or her crib — the world of your toes, your fingers, your mother's nipple, your wet feeling, pain, pleasure. But the infant finally leaves the crib and moves about the living room or other parts of the house, and then down the block, to kindergarten, grammar school, i.e., into the world mediated by meaning.

The world mediated by meaning is the world in which most adults live. In the world mediated by meaning, however, there are at least two very special and very different worlds. I have already alluded to them: the world of common sense and the world of theory. The world of common sense is basically what the Greeks called the world of mythos. It is the world of description. The world of theory is the world of logos, the world of discursive reasoning, which we have heard chided somewhat during these deliberations. Another distinction sometimes made within the world mediated by meaning, and frequently accompanied by connotations of incompatibility, is that made between the world of science and technology and the world of religion.

All of them, however, deal with meaning. And most people, because they do not differentiate the different worlds, cut off one or the other in order to be comfortable in the house in which they abide. They sever their relationship with one or the other because of a certain cognitive, aesthetic, emotional, or sociological disfunctioning, a certain dis-ease that they encounter when they move from one world to another world.

Human consciousness is complex. It is often undifferentiated and it is polymorphic, when one is serving a local community in the functional specialty, communication. That is why the last presentation was so excellent. The speaker had a good background in the various aspects of this process, but had the art and skill of translating it by means of the functional specialty of communication in his context of St. Thomas' parish. That is not something one does randomly at an occasional parish meeting. It is an art that is partly cultivated, partly inherited, and partly gift.

Because human consciousness is so complex, and because many people do not normally differentiate and personally appropriate the many dimensions of human consciousness, there occurs a further problematic situation — the fact that the many carriers of meaning are sometimes confused. The entire process I am discussing is concerned with human consciousness and dealing with meaning.

The history of the church has been the mediation of meaning from a past context to a present context, in order to illuminate life today and to give hope for the future. What has been mediated, we hope, is the paradigmatic life, ministry and death of Jesus of Nazareth, exalted as the Christ, as the disclosing symbol of God's abiding presence within the mystery of human existence.

But the carriers of meaning are many. The carriers of meaning are subjectivity, emotion, feeling, art, symbol, ritual, language. And language may be technical, or literary, or common sense. The carrier of meaning that is inter-subjectivity is the one that we know most readily. Many of us are strangers — we have never met before. But there is a certain inter-subjectivity, a certain recognition that a wink, a nod, a smile arouses. It communicates my interiority to you even though I do not know you. There is this world of inter-subjectivity where meaning inside of me can become meaning inside of you.

There is also the world of meaning of my own interior emotions and feelings, sometimes so deep that Jung and others have called them subconscious and unconscious. That interior world can overflow in expressions of art, ritual, symbol, etc. When it overflows in these ways, particularly if it thereby becomes an interpretative scheme of the meaning of life, it may be seen as mythopoeic.

Meaning also takes the form of language. It can become the language of common sense: the sun rises and sets. Or, it can become technical language: the earth moves in an elliptical circle around the sun. It can be descriptive language: Jesus is Lord; Jesus is the messiah; Jesus is the suffering servant; Jesus is the high priest. Or it can attempt to be definitional language: Jesus enjoys a divine person, and a human and a divine nature. Language has that peculiarity of splitting off into two or three forms: common sense descriptive language; literary, self-involving language; technical language.

Technical language is particularly significant for us, because, for good or evil, the Western Christian church has tended to try to mediate its meaning from the past context to the present context by means of a technical language, in which certain control of meaning was operative, every single word had very specific meaning, so that anyone who studied the technical language would gain, more or less, the same set of insights.

Because of this historical tendency, technical language has had a preeminence in the Western church. Precisely defined, dogmatic connotations are characteristic, and one had to know Greek philosophy to fully understand christological and trinitarian statements. There was a bias that suggested that other language expressions, other carriers of meaning, could not mediate this reality, because they might lack the same control of meaning. For my part, I am not so sure that they can, but that is a disputed question.

Over and above inter-subjectivity, emotion, affective feeling, art, symbol, ritual, language, there is also incarnate meaning. Incarnate meaning is what happens when you encounter a Mother Theresa of Calcutta, or a Martin Luther King, or a John XXIII — when you encounter one whose self-consistency in word and deed is so genuine that it is not possible to doubt one is encountering an authentic self.

There is no doubt. The truth is incarnate. There is no need to get into arguments and theories and credentials. The meaning is incarnate in the concrete person.

Now, theologically and liturgically, in terms of the concerns of this conference, where does all this lead? It leads to each one of us as one seeking to be an instance of authentic incarnate meaning. Each of us is seeking an interior harmony — a harmony of our feelings, our theoretical understandings, our symbols and dreams. We are seeking a personal integration, a person synthesis. Ordinarily religion and therefore liturgy play an important role in one's interior harmony. But there are often tensions, particularly in a period of rapid change like the present.

It is very difficult to maintain a full harmony among these several dimensions because, for example, in the psychic world the human spirit is impelled into mystery, into the unknown. We encounter the horizon of more questions than we can answer. Not in the sense of technical problems, which can be solved in time with patience and perseverance, but in the sense of radical, impenetrable mystery.

When one meets the unknown, or mystery, there are different ways of dealing with it. One way is the emergence of a mythopoeic world view as a symbol system for interpreting reality. Jung, Ricoeur, Eliade and others have examined this phenomenon. There are times when the mythopoeic symbols deal with a depth dimension of human existence that cannot be expressed in any other way, but there are other times when they serve as a stop-gap measure for a more exact form of understanding.

Before people knew about volcanoes, it was easy to say that the god is rumbling on the mountain in his wrath. Eventually, however, culture forces a change and one interpretation gives way to another. Once one knows about volcanoes, one need no longer reverence the mountain as the seat of deity.

In the context of the world of aesthetics, look at the martyrology of the Christmas liturgy. It proclaims that Jesus Christ was born when the whole universe was in harmonious expectation. Now we can see that all of that is a literary form. There was nothing special about the time when Jesus was born. No evidence suggests that the universe was in a state of cosmic serenity. Indeed, from a Teilhardian point of view, one might ask whether Jesus should have come at that time or should be yet to come. The nativity narrative has traditionally been proclaimed with drama and pageantry in Christmas liturgies. What does one do with the fact that, on the cognitive level, theologians and exegetes have all but concluded that the Lucan narrative of the birth of Jesus is a midrash. It is not a literal, factual event.

This does not mean it is meaningless. It is a carrier of meaning, but not a carrier of cognitive historical information, any more than the cosmology of the creation of the world in Genesis is cognitive, factual, scientific information. It is meaningful and it is even quite true, but not in a literal sense.

What does one do, liturgically, when the functional specialty of communication is dealing with undifferentiated human consciousness, and therefore to tell the people that something is not literally true may mean for them that it is not meaningful? This is a very difficult and delicate situation because it deals with what people consider to be the core truths of their lives. It is asking a great deal of ordinary people with no formal training to maintain a religious equilibrium when their daily lived experience suggests one religious vision (existential mediation), the theologians in the universities armed with the historical critical method suggest another, and the bishops from the authority of their office suggest yet another (dogmatic mediation).

During such a difficult juncture (in the midst of a knowledge explosion that defies anyone to get on top of all there is to be learned), one could hope for some solace from the uplifting ritual action of the liturgy. However, as we shall now see, the present ferment has raised the question: "What is liturgy celebrating, anyway?"

What is liturgy celebrating?

What is liturgy celebrating, anyway? This question is problematic. When we examine what is going on in the church, we find that there are a great many possible answers to that question. Liturgy could be celebrating the peaks and valleys of human experience — high points and low points, happiness, sadness, grief and renewal. Liturgy could be celebrating rites of passage in human life: birth, maturity (with commitments to marriage or other vocation), death. Clearly the sacraments correspond to the moments of passage or trauma in the human adventure. Liturgy could be celebrating the universal human need for healing, reconciliation, binding, purging, transforming. However, if liturgy is celebrating only these realities, then some of the Christian symbols are helpful but others are not, and some are simply embarrassing.

Another possibility, of course, is that liturgy embraces all of this and more by celebrating a paradigmatic event, an event that transforms three categories of sacred time: the past, the present and the future. The event of the life of Jesus of Nazareth who was born, lived, taught, ministered, suffered, was put to death, transcended death paradoxically and was proclaimed and exalted as the Christ — that is celebrated in liturgy in such a way that its interpretation of the past event has a plenitude of meaning for the present. That past event becomes sacred time. "In illo tempore" is different from any of the great mythological statements identifying sacred time, and different from the fairy tale designation of "once upon a time," because of an affirmed historical component.

"In illo tempore" a plenitude of meaning occurred, which grounds the possibility of having meaning and hope and joy in the present. Just as it celebrates the affirmation of a meaningful and usable future. As someone has pointed out, however, this gets factored off into all kind of symbol systems and pious traditions and devotions — into a variety of phenomena that may be more socio-cultural than they are theological or liturgical or worshipful.

What happens when the question of what liturgy is mediating is put into these contexts? Dogmatically, liturgy is celebrating the cognitive content of one's religious self-understanding. Liturgy must preserve then a certain cognitive content. So the words become very important and the liturgy cannot depart from certain words. This problem is evident in any highly articulated liturgical or theological tradition. It is extremely obvious in any discussion of Roman Catholic liturgical celebrations. This is why a decade ago few could believe that the Roman canon would ever be prayed aloud in the vernacular. After that happened, few could believe that other eucharistic prayers would be added. When three more were added, it was said that that was the end and there could be no more. Then there emerged experimental and underground liturgy books, and reactions against "illicit" liturgical expressions. Nevertheless, a complex and, we must admit it, sometimes irresponsible, developmental process is at work, and no mere juridical procedure can stop it.

We should not be surprised at the present tension between local and universal church in the effort to adapt liturgical celebrations to national, racial and ethnic particularities without further loss of a more fundamental religious self-concept. You can be sure that some of the caution about experimental centers for an American Black liturgy are based on the fear that the church's worship will be "used" to celebrate Black pride and not the Christ-event. Of course, a tour of the ethnic parishes in any large American city would reveal that the Christ event is already wedded to many ethnic identities.

Questions for collaboration

To conclude, I have several questions to suggest for our ongoing collaboration. I have mentioned some of them already. Who is the accrediting agency for genuine Blackness? Are middle-class values intrinsically White values? Are many of the Black and White distinctions that have been made in our colloquium more socio-cultural and economic than they are racial or ethnic?

I remember an ecumenical study on religion in Chicago which we conducted a few years ago. One of the things we discovered was that differences concerning types and styles of liturgical celebration — whether the respondents were Black or White, Methodist, Catholic, Lutheran, Anglican, or Baptist — seemed to be related to sociocultural and economic characteristics rather than to racial or religious ones. What does that mean?

To move on to the question I consider to be the most difficult of all: is it possible, once a people becomes self-conscious about its ritual-making nature, to systematically change and create rituals by Vatican fiat or by liturgical commissions? Formerly, when peoples were not so conscious, rituals and myths and symbol systems moved through a culture like electricity. They moved like water through the land and through the earth — now a nice growth, now a dead end, now a beautiful plumage.

There was no way of stopping the process, abstracting the meaning as if it were independent of the ritual. Is it possible to do this now? Can we distill profound religious symbols from one context and insert them into another by self-conscious experimentation? What do we think that an authentic Afro-American Catholic liturgy would look like?

I applaud what this conference is doing and I am happy to have been with you. I do not wish to disenchant you or to deter you from your important work by anything that I have said. In one of his more descriptive passages, in *Insight,* Bernard Lonergan wrote this paragraph: "Thales was so intent upon the stars that he did not see the well into which he tumbled. The milkmaid was so indifferent to the stars that she could not overlook the well. Still, Thales could have seen the well, for, after all, he was not blind. And, perhaps, the milkmaid could have been interested in the stars, for she was human."

Even though I am fond of star-gazing, I hope that I am sufficiently human to be concerned about the well — especially since, it appears, we are in need of a new one. Or, to return to the image with which I began: know that I am very fond of weavers of baskets even though for the present, at least, I am cast as a blower of glass.

LITURGICAL PRACTICE IN THE BLACK PARISH: ST. BENEDICT THE MOOR

William L. Norvel

Dealing with history and fears

When I became its pastor in 1975, St. Benedict the Moor parish in Northeast Washington, D.C. was celebrating its 25th anniversary. It was and is a lower middle class Black church, and I know that my coming dampened the ardor of its celebration. It didn't quite know how to deal with the new Black pastor.

A lot of buried middle-class fears began to surface. Some said frankly, "We don't want a Black pastor." Some were suspicious that the advent of a Black man in that role would mean "bringing all of that Black stuff into our parish." The practical types said, "We will go under financially. Our school will fall apart. And there will be a swarm of new Black people coming into the parish, people who haven't been part of us."

Although there were many welcomes, there were also many greetings that cloaked real fears. When they saw that I was young, they were quite sure that Fr. Mullowney would be back in another year. Things were very, very difficult for a time, and I tried to play it cool.

I began with a heavy schedule of pastoral visits. I did this in order to feel them out, to deal with their fears, to show them that I was taking those fears seriously (because they were serious). After all, the people in that parish had built a good community in a place that was formerly the city dump. That is where the city had put them long ago, and they had worked hard to build good homes and to improve the area tremendously.

It was not hard to understand the fears — the fear, for example, that all that they had so carefully built up might be lost. So I listened, listened well. To the old timers, my youth made me a little boy, and I gained much wisdom from their counsel. They told me of the heartaches, the pain they had suffered at the hands of other Catholics and their clergy. Every one of them could relate experiences of being kicked out of or rejected by the (White) Catholic churches that surrounded their community. They had been told again and again that they were not wanted, that they should go to "their own" Black churches, at a time when there were only a couple of Black parishes in the city. They were not welcome in "White churches," and there was no doubt about it.

Because the churches around them would not accept them, they built on that city dump a parish plant which would minister to their spiritual, social and recreational needs. St. Benedict's takes a particular pride in the fact that it paid for its construction and maintenance without seeking subsidies from the archdiocese. As a matter of fact, the parish has been in a position to loan the archdiocese $50,000. There is a fierce pride that still dominates the spirit of all of the original parishioners.

One of the old timers said something I have remembered: "Father, I am 75 years old. Excuse the language, but I know you're getting a lot of hell here. But I have been waiting for a Black priest all my life, so, please, don't leave!"

A community of many gifts

At any rate, I listened and tried to discern their feelings and what lay behind them. It soon became quite clear to me that my basic task (I suppose it is the basic task of any pastor anywhere) was to build a Christian community. And that meant trying to open up all the present members of the parish to the wider community, the whole community. I suppose that, too, was somewhat threatening to a group that had felt forced to protect itself in enclave fashion.

No one darker than myself, for example, had any position of leadership in the parish. Youth had not been welcomed. Old people had been made to feel that they had done their duty and should now lay down and die. Only the middle class and the middle aged were really operating the parish.

To bring all of the people together, to develop a real Christian love for and openness to everyone in the larger community — Catholic or not, old, middle aged and young — was a tremendously difficult challenge. We had to start by finding Black leadership in the parish at all levels.

And there were other things, other ruts, other established patterns in the way: there were cliques, there was an established power structure, there was an unwillingness to share. We approached the task cautiously. My religious superior sent an associate, a man who had been my rector in the seminary, and the first thing we did together was to develop a fairly complete overview of the parish and diocese. With that in mind, we started determining how we were going to plan and program the kind of community building we needed.

The plan would have to be articulated in every phase of parish life and in every aspect of pastoral activity, and always in a Black context. Beneath the surface of most of the people — as I discovered during those pastoral visits — their experiences had been very much the same as those of my own parents. They had worked in the kitchens of the White folk, and they had occupied lower positions in the White House and the government buildings of the city. But with their relative prosperity they had suppressed all that. In many ways and for many reasons, they had lost sight of it.

Cultivating Black awareness

I wanted to bring all of this forward and get it out again in plain sight. Because those experiences were a real part of those people, experiences that had brought them this far, experiences which their children should understand and should feel they are a part of. We began to talk about those experiences in homilies, and some began to make the connection: "Why are our children leaving the church? Why are they disowning us?"

We told them, "You have 'protected' your children by cutting them off from Black experience in America. They leave your home and community for college and they come face to face for the first time with what it means to be Black in this country and they can't handle it. Therefore, they have difficulty dealing with you." The message was repeated in various modes, in homilies, in parish communications generally.

I found some people who were willing to work with me and we set about reorganizing the community and setting up a parish council. After a while, I got brave enough to place some banner-mottoes on the walls of the church building: "Black is not a color but an experience" and "God in his wisdom has made me Black and beautiful."

When the congregation saw those banners the next Sunday, all hell broke loose. One could feel, almost tangibly, a tension and antagonism and the gathering of forces. We had scheduled the first parish council meeting for the following Sunday, so I began to anticipate the bodies and the ammunition that would be marshaled for the event. We had a full church for that parish council meeting — a phenomenon which has never been repeated since.

By that time, I knew where they were coming from and what they would ask. I just let them go at me for a while until most of the questions and most of the fears had been exposed. Then I began to ask some loaded questions, and there was dialogue. I passed out some papers which had been prepared to deal with a number of their anticipated objections. For an hour and a half we tried to deal with them, and that was a very important period in the delivery process of a new St. Benedict the Moor parish.

After voicing their complaints, they did listen. They still had lots of questions. They didn't agree with everything about the concept of Blackness we had been promoting: that we were going to be a Black church, develop a Black awareness, incorporate into our liturgies Black elements, encourage Black leadership.

We pointed out that the church is starving for these Black gifts. They are here and we are not ready to share them. So we have to open ourselves up to the needs of the entire community in which the church is situated. This church is here to serve a community.

Mutinies and bounties

After it was all over, a woman who had been queen of the parish for many years stood up and asked: "Do you mean to tell me that those banners are going to stay on the wall?" I answered, "Yes, ma'am, as long as I am pastor." She said, "Well, I'm leaving and I won't be back, and I refuse to participate in anything any more in this parish!" As she swept out, another woman shouted after her, "Bye now!" St. Benedict the Moor had set a new direction for itself.

That wasn't the end of the struggle, but I think it was the critical turning point. Some said, "All right. We'll give you the benefit of the doubt. We'll go with you. You lead us." But others started a campaign to boycott giving to the church's collections. "We'll teach him. We won't contribute." There was a parish raffle going on at the time and some vowed: "Okay, we'll do it this way. We won't sell our raffle books."

I was well acquainted by then with almost everyone, so I knew what was going on and who was involved. I asked fifteen people who comprised a kind of core group of objection and dissent to come in one evening for a meeting. They did not know its purpose, but they came. After they were seated, I spoke very frankly about the destructive things they had been doing and about the harm and ugliness of divisiveness. I told them I did not appreciate their efforts to stop contributions. I told them that, if they could not join in a common effort, they should feel free to leave the parish, but that we would like to have them join and to help and to cease obstructing.

They were surprised by this direct approach, but they could not deny facts which I had carefully ascertained before the meeting. Two of them left the parish, as a result, but later returned. A last ditch effort was made to divide the two priests. My associate was older than I and White, so some thought that they could play one of us against the other. The associate did not permit that effort to get off the ground, by making it quite clear that he was with the pastor.

Since then there has been a generally positive thrust. This has been facilitated by our being aware of their fears and being willing to deal with them in an understanding and non-embarrassing way. Liturgical celebration has been the center of our efforts — it has been, in other words, where it should be. We keep saying, in one way and another, that there is another way of being Black — a way different from the way of fear and suppression and embarrassment.

We emphasize that we can be proud of our Blackness, and that the liturgy is the place where we celebrate that pride and that beautiful Black experience. There, in liturgy, Christ meets that experience, graces it with meaning and a sense of direction. These are the kinds of themes we have tried to develop in our early efforts.

Getting ourselves together

The value of fellowship and closeness and neighborliness for the development of genuine community has been stressed again and again. I used to say on Sundays: "We come to mass to celebrate. We come to mass to help carry one another's burdens. But we are not yet doing these things here. You are too quiet. You don't even speak to each other. Many of you don't know each other."

The presiders at Sunday liturgy tried to crack the ice. We would say, from the altar: "Good morning, Mary, how are you this morning?" And again the fear and the embarrassment would be evident. But, after a while, Mary started answering: "Good morning, Father." And that simple kind of sharing led us to explore gradually how necessary other, deeper ways of sharing and getting to know one another are, if worship is to involve a community rather than merely a group of individuals. If we are there to worship and to bear each other's burdens, then we have to share, we have to bring our joy, our happiness, our fears, our whole selves and lives into the action.

It took a while to begin to make a dent in long established practices and customs. "Father, you just don't speak out in front of the Blessed Sacrament. You must be 'reverent.'" So I would ask, "Do we have a God who is stuck-up and remote? I bet God loves to hear us tell each other how we are. God is interested in knowing that you want to know how John is, because John is sick and is not here."

It has taken time, but when the congregation gathers for mass now it is a family. Most of them know when a certain person is not present, and they will go to the partner or a family member or close friend and ask, "Where is Mary?" "Where is John?" The greeting has been restored. They are in a mood to worship. They are trying to bring their whole selves into the action. If there is any sickness, a death, a pain, it comes out there because there is sharing. These things are articulated in the prayer of the faithful and at the handshake of peace.

The idea of the parish, the local church as a minister to the total community and city means that we have to serve, we have to go out and meet the dope addict. We have to be concerned with the prostitute on Benning Road. We have to reach out to young people who are not coming to mass and who are not in school. We have to be in touch with D. C. Jail, and go there, and see our sisters and brothers.

Community building is an earthy business — very concrete, very messy. Sisters and brothers occur only in particular and in the flesh. Therefore, social justice and social concerns are never absent from our preaching, and there are signs of progress here, as well. Now we have a group anxious to go the the D. C. Jail and to Lorton (another correctional institution) — not just to bring goodies, but to participate, to share, to celebrate liturgy. We have a youth committee that is strong and committed. We have a lot of "outsiders," as well as our own parish members, participating in social events, spiritual events, retreats.

And the community emphasis has been joined by a revival of a desire to witness. If one believes in Jesus Christ as Savior, and that he has called us together in a worshiping community, one has to give witness to that gift. In a number of different ways that witness is gradually becoming manifest, both in liturgical celebrations and elsewhere.

We are still working on the development of Black leadership, still working to encourage people to think original thoughts and to take original initiatives. Catholic training has been effective in creating a tendency to wait for Father's ideas and Father's direction, to do nothing unless Father says so. In time past, we fostered those attitudes and, unfortunately, we were more successful in that fostering than we were in pursuing some of our other, more praiseworthy goals.

In cultivating leadership, it is crucial that at some point the clergy sit back and let others carry the ball. An experience I have had in the last few days has been a beautiful example of this. Our parish is planning to build a million dollar community center. Naturally, they had been waiting for "Father" to show them how to go about getting more money collected for the purpose.

But I said to them, "Father's done his work. As a matter of fact, Father is going to New York with his sister for three days. I hope that when I return everything will be ready both for the groundbreaking ceremony and the building fund program." I went, and when I came back yesterday I found that they had made all arrangements for the groundbreaking and they had produced a plan for getting more pledges for the building fund. They are all involved, and that is all it takes.

A struggle for gospel song

One of my most cherished dreams has always been to bring into our eucharistic celebrations what I feel is going to be the major Black contribution to Catholicism: a warmth of fellowship and of concern for one another, and a real sense of celebration of the word and of the sacrament.

I have felt for some time that one of the ways that this could best be done is by developing a gospel choir. I think we need a compelling gospel music woven into the fabric of eucharistic celebration, enhancing it, illustrating it, enabling the Black religious experience that I have longed for all my life.

When I first asked the people to form a gospel choir, they laughed. "Don't tell us you're now going to try to bring that gospel music into the church!" And I could understand the lack of sympathy. I had gone through — down in Mississippi — elementary school, high school, years and years of seminary training, without ever having gained the slightest appreciation for any form of Black awareness . . . and certainly none for Black gospel music. I knew where they were coming from.

But there was a former member of St. Benedict the Moor, who had joined a Baptist church because nothing was happening at home, and who was an associate director of the Howard University Gospel Choir. I asked him to come back and help me start a gospel choir. He returned for two weeks, but when six people turned up for practice, he said, "Father, I beg you, hold me excused." And he returned whence he came.

It seemed impossible, but we kept on trying. I found a man by the name of the Reverend Ezekiel Thomas, of the Bible Way Baptist Church in this city. I asked, "Zeke, will you help me?" And Zeke did. He pulled a group together in our parish, helped them lose some of their inhibitions and embarrassments and fears, got them going.

Finally, they had their big day. They were ready to sing for a Sunday mass. They came in and they walked down the aisle and took their places, looking very nice. But one could hardly hear them during the celebration, so fearful were they of opening their mouths and putting a little soul into their song. Zeke, on the other hand, was going to town on the piano and the organ. We had Zeke with us for a year and he brought that choir a long, long way. It was such a good experience for Zeke that he not only played better than ever, but at times would get carried away, jump up and do a holy dance.

I told him, "Wait a minute, Zeke! You're going to kill my whole program. They just are not ready for that!" But it was like talking to a wall. In fact, one time Zeke got up and actually tried to walk the wall. People were frightened, and it ruined the service. They were not ready, emotionally, psychologically, spiritually, to sympathize with that kind of ecstatic behavior. Some stopped coming, saying, "It looks like a Baptist church." I just couldn't get Zeke to control the spirit for a while to let them grow in it. So I had to get rid of Zeke.

Fortunately, I found our present director, Mr. Ronald Harbor, who has a beautiful sense of where the people are, of how to work together in bringing them to a greater appreciation of the Black gospel tradition, and of presenting a music that enhances the celebration of the eucharist. We work together at Saturday evening rehearsals — I talk about the Sunday texts and my preaching theme, Ronald sits down at the piano and makes the appropriate music come out, and the choir catches on and begins to open up.

A one week workshop with Avon Gillespie was a decisive element in the transformation. He took them back to their childhood, with rhymes and games and play, in a way that brought home a host of recollections. Then he asked them where they learned these things. "My grandmother taught it to me." "Where did your grandmother get it?" And he led them back to Africa in a very natural, game-recalling, play-recalling way. At the end of the week he brought them (and all they had been doing and experiencing) together in a liturgical celebration. That was really the birth of our gospel choir.

The gospel choir is now forty strong and sings at the 10:30 mass on Sundays. We kept the 12:15 mass for those whom I knew would never move toward gospel music. I had no wish to change them.

Our young people are chips off the old blocks and have been in some ways more difficult to communicate with than their parents. Originally, I tried to develop a gospel choir for the youth of the parish, also. But they stayed away in droves and wanted nothing to do with it. It is a long story, but there has been dialogue and progress has been made. Now there is a youth choir, and it is a gospel choir, and they sing at the 9 a.m. children's or family mass. They call themselves "The Reflections of Faith." Mr. Harbor developed the group, which numbers 35 or more at this time. At that celebration, young people not only do the singing but also do the reading, ushering, serving and liturgical dancing. Children we haven't seen in years are coming to that mass and identifying with it.

At the 7 a.m. celebration, we give the old timers four hymns, and a chance for confession before mass. These various types of celebration help the parish function in a changing time and enable some other developments and progress to proceed — for example, the encouragment of Black leadership. They bring in everyone and provide a base from which everyone can work together toward common goals.

An immediate goal is the construction of a community center. The old timers really wanted to build a "church." Some others were saying, "We need a place in which to gather, to have our social and community activities." So I asked them to call a meeting, sit down together and determine what we should do. They did that.

The parish council had been working long enough to have a steady finger on the pulse of the parish and to know the real needs of the people fairly well. The old timers came with their views and were very articulate. Eventually, they jointly determined that we needed a community center. They decided that the building we have now can be made into a permanent church structure later on. "These are our needs," they said. "These are the needs of the community." And it was a common decision, a consensus.

We still have a long, long way to go, and we at St. Benedict the Moor are working at it. I am very proud of the distance we have come. Some of the priests were placing bets when I first came to the parish: "He'll be out in a year!" They are not betting any more. We organized the first church-affiliated gospel choir and gospel mass in this archdiocese. Our Sunday liturgies are well attended. We are reclaiming Black Catholics who have been out of the church for five, ten, fifteen, twenty-five years. People are coming to worship with us from as far away as Baltimore.

Some have said encouraging things when I have asked them why they have joined us, or have returned: "I've been coming here for many Sundays, trying to see if there is real consistency in your talk about Black awareness and your development of Black leadership, trying to see if you really mean it."

Before the ministry of reconciliation can reach out as effectively as it should, it must reach within each Catholic to rediscover the richness of a heritage. Before the world can be embraced, we have to go inside ourselves, discover the gifts we have, develop those gifts, use them, celebrate them, live them. This is what we have been trying to do thus far at St. Benedict the Moor.

LITURGICAL PRACTICE IN THE BLACK PARISH: ST. FRANCIS XAVIER

Henry J. Offer

Singing and enjoying

Let me add to this practical, pastoral side of the discussion as much as I can from the perspective of a White priest, ordained 33 years, whose ministry has been entirely in the Black community: five years in Texas, five in Detroit, and 23 in two parishes in Baltimore. My present parish is the oldest Black Catholic congregation in the United States. It dates from 1863.

I do not have answers to relate, but I have experiences to share. I used to think that I knew a whole lot about the people I was serving. Now I am convinced that I have learned more about them in the last seven or eight — or maybe ten — years than I learned in all the previous ones. And I still have problems. Every time I come upon a solution, I discover two new problems.

Interest in gospel singing in our parish began in 1970. We heard something about a parish in New Orleans — St. Francis De Sales. A Black priest who was traveling through Baltimore spoke of its gospel choir and the tremendous effect it was having on parish liturgies. He was personally unconvinced, but he told us: "If this is reaching people, you know, maybe it's a good way to go."

At that time I knew next to nothing about Black music in general or about gospel music in particular. It was a difficult year in the city (and in the country). Spirits were low. Feelings of frustration were high. Even though the Black Caucus had taken over the pulpit one Sunday, perception of the church's role in all the ferment and unhappiness was unclear.

The other priest in the parish at the time, Philip Linden, got the idea and invited a musician from New Orleans to spend two weeks with us, to try to get the choir started. I joined in, not knowing exactly why, and shared the work of promotion and of implementation.

On one Sunday, we asked the congregation: "Who would like to join a gospel choir?" On cards provided, 85 people signed up and said they would. When the gentleman from New Orleans arrived, 45 showed up for the first practice, and we had one applicant for the job of director. They practiced every night, and we had a choir at mass the very next Sunday. I didn't know they needed to face the congregation when they sang, so I was quite surprised when suddenly there they were — 67 singers all around me at the altar.

It seems strange, but it is a true confession: after spending a quarter of a century in ministry in the Black community, that event was really the beginning of my realization of what the Black experience in music is about. We have had a gospel choir at that mass every Sunday since that day. Now we have two choirs — regularly about 35 singers in that one, and a younger choir of 20 that sings at another mass. The latter sings gospel music, too, but in a slightly different style.

Watching and working to get this process started impressed me deeply. To see all those people signing up so quickly, coming out night after night during those first two weeks, and enjoying it all so much — it was an eye-opener. I am not saying that it was all easy from then on. There are always problems and they are different in every parish. But, without some price, some pain, some anguish, nothing good ever happens . . . because good things do not just "happen" — they are created.

Fr. Clarence Rivers has worked with our choirs and with several other choral groups at a workshop in our church. He can tell you something about the pain and the anguish. For the concerts following that workshop, we filled the church twice and had 155 singers. And I remember well Fr. Rivers's point about not being afraid if we find worship entertaining. Liturgical celebrations should be enjoyable, he said, and if they are not they are bad celebrations.

Some of our people were unhappy, of course. "Well, *they* come to church just to see a show!" Frankly, I don't care why they come. I really don't. I just want them to come. Once they are there, then it is our obligation and our privilege to do everything we can to enable a good worship experience, a good experience of common prayer. And we take that job seriously.

Proclaiming and preaching

We spend a lot of time on our preaching. And we have developed a fairly large number of good proclaimers, good readers. We know how long it takes to find them and then to train them — so that they are not simply *reading*. We want them to *proclaim* the readings. It makes a big difference in the congregation's experience. The music is important. The proclaiming is important. The preaching is important.

None of it can happen without Black leadership and without a certain willingness to go with it, to run with it, even to be swept off one's feet at times. We had one choir director who had them dancing down the aisle — and it was appropriate and it was moving. I remember how frightened some were when somebody started clapping one Sunday. "Oh, we'd better not clap in church!" It took us a while. But the results have been as good for the solidarity of the parish as they have been for its spirit.

Now, if one examines the congregation at either of the Sunday masses in which our gospel choirs sing, one can see no sign of an age or class division. Both congregations give every evidence of being good cross sections of the parish, with people of every age and of many different backgrounds participating and enjoying.

We sometimes feel a bit constricted and would like to have more freedom for liturgical adaptation, and that, I think, is a sign of progress. Whether that constriction is a matter of law or a matter of our habits and customs, it is good for us to realize that we are still in the early stages of a profound renewal. It will be a long time before we are free enough to be more concerned with the purpose of ritual structures than we are with their details.

I suspect the big event of Sunday mass in our parish these days is the peace greeting. We really tear the church apart in those moments. We sing. The clergy go down the aisle. When I come back up, I feel ready for holy communion. At times, a visiting priest has volunteered the opinion that we overdo it, but I don't think so. The exchange, the warmth, the moving about combine to produce a good atmosphere — a feeling of being together, or, at least, wanting to be together.

Even if we are not as together as we would like to be, we are trying to build community in our parish. And the reaching for it, the gesture that indicates a hunger for it is a beautiful thing. We are not yet generally strong in congregational participation in liturgical celebration, and it is this kind of good participatory experience that will help us along the way.

Learning from the Baptists

Another experience that I have lately found to be extremely valuable is a sharing in and study of the various styles we find in other Black churches of other traditions — specifically, Baptist churches. I wish I had known that when I was ordained. I wouldn't have wasted so much time. I think I would have spent a lot of time profitably by going from Baptist church to Baptist church, participating in the services, listening, feeling, sensing — the style of music, the style of preaching, the style of praying.

We invited the leading Baptist preacher in town to lead a revival in our church last May. The first night we had 350 people, the second night 570, the last night more than a thousand. I am not suggesting that anyone should merely copy or slavishly imitate someone else's style. I know that I have to be myself to function effectively as a leader of worship. I cannot pretend to be other than I am. I do not come out of the Black experience, for example, so I should not pretend that I do.

But I can be at home with that experience. And I can learn a great deal from these styles and practices about communicating within the realm of that experience. I can find new ways of relating to people and, without copying anybody's style, can begin to feel and sense subtle values and responsive chords that may vastly improve my ministry.

Black artists have helped us with the use of color and form in worship and in the decoration of the worship environment. For our church renovation we went to professionals who transformed a building I had thought absolutely impossible into a marvelous worship space. We do a Black calendar, geared to Baltimore, which tries to spotlight the talents of the people of the community that we serve. The idea behind the calendar was to help raise the sights of people — to help them see that there is a lot of talent in their community and city. Perhaps, then, they will look at themselves and begin to discover how gifted they are.

These are a few indications of the ways in which we have been operating at St. Francis Xavier. Being attentive to experiences, learning from experiences, and engaging in a constant search — these are the ways we have found we have to go if we are to be pastorally effective. We have to be real and everything we do has to be real — nothing fraudulent, nothing fake, nothing phony. Only if we are real can we get in touch with others through the experiences that mean something to them. And then the search. I am still searching, and I think we all have to keep on searching.

MUSIC IN THE BLACK SPIRITUAL TRADITION

Grayson W. Brown

Principal role or "extra"?

The history of the importance of music in the Black tradition is a very important history, but it is also one that involves much detail that is irrelevant to our particular concerns here. Instead of tracing that history, I am going to discuss my own experience of growing up in a Black community and of what music has meant in surviving (and thriving) in that Black community.

Music is terribly important, vital, central to us and in our lives. That is fundamental. And it is not as obvious as it sounds — especially for us in the Catholic tradition. I have been a Catholic church organist for fifteen years. I have planned, participated in, played for hundreds and hundreds of liturgical celebrations — not only in my home parish but all over the country. God has smiled on me, and I've had a chance to do some traveling.

Everywhere I go I find scenes pretty much the same, at least in one respect. Liturgy planning group meetings are predictable. A priest, some sisters, maybe a deacon, one or two people from the congregation (despite their preponderance in numbers, these last appear more rarely in these roles) sit around, looking at the readings — say, for a Sunday in Lent —, drawing out a theme, homilizing about it, paying a bit of attention to the other parts of the liturgy whenever it is a question of the words to be used. That takes up about 99% of the available time. Then at the very end when they have (as they would claim) "planned the celebration," someone says: "It might be nice if we could throw in a few hymns. Anything we can sing? Anything Lenty, you know?"

That sort of thing drives me absolutely crazy. Music in the Black spiritual tradition is not an extra, not frosting, not simply a refreshing interlude in the action, not something one "throws in." Music is part of the very heart of celebration. It's at the center of things — not an afterthought. It is not a moment of pleasure tucked in between the serious parts. It is not even a means of entertainment for a bored congregation. It is entertaining in the sense that it is involving, it is a means by which we participate, and it makes us feel good in doing so.

I have heard Black preachers say that if anyone were to come to them and ask them to have a service without music, they could not do it. If you were to say to a Black preacher: "We want you to help us with a celebration, but we don't have much time. Can we just go ahead with the rite as it is in the books and maybe sing one song at the beginning and one at the end?" — he could not do that. He could not do it because his people would not let him do it and because in that event he would not even feel as if he were celebrating.

Affective epistemology

Whatever we can say of other groups and cultures, Black people are people who are greatly affected by emotional experience. The impact of experience on us is the impact of feelings as well as ideas. If an experience causes us to feel something, it has impact — and the impact cannot be articulated by mere words. Sometimes indeed it is difficult to communicate it at all.

I know that I may be on dangerous and controversial ground when I say these things. What I am talking about can be described as an affective epistemology. For example, I met Brother Joe Davis when he returned from a trip to Africa. It was evident in a number of ways that he had been profoundly affected by his stay there. I said, "Joe, how was your trip?"

Joseph is an extremely articulate man, but he stumbled and reached for words. He said, "Well, it was beautiful. It was more than beautiful — it was . . . well, it's really hard to talk about it." I would guess that if, at that moment, everyone in the room had stood and had sung "Lift Every Voice and Sing," Joseph would have been able to communicate in song what that "going home" had meant to him.

We are a very religious people, for at least two reasons. Firstly, in our African heritage, religion is synonymous with life, inseparable from any aspect of human development or activity or culture. It was reflected in *Roots,* when the father raised the newborn child to heaven saying, "Behold, the only thing greater than yourself."

Secondly, we arrived in America as slaves. Slaves *have* to believe. The God-oriented and mystery-oriented culture of Africa became an urgent imperative for slaves in America. We had to believe in a God who was very real and very close to us. God had to be at least as real for us as were the miseries of slavery and depression. We could not afford a distant deity. If every day is a life and death struggle, God has to be there. God has to be close. God has to be that which one can touch and, for an affective people, that which one can feel.

In the Black spiritual tradition, music is a vehicle which permits me to move from the frustration of trying to express something by inadequate means to the point where I can express something in a satisfying way, from deep down inside, comfortably and freely. Music brings me to that point. Music enables that kind of expression. It is that step beyond inadequacy.

Black preachers know this well. I assume everyone has heard a Black preacher somewhere sometime. He is really into delivering the word of God and he is feeling it. He starts off slowly. He talks and he listens for the encouragement of the people in the congregation whose feelings are being stirred, too. He begins to build up his sermon . . . and eventually he may break into song.

I don't mean that he will sing a distinguishable melody. How does he sing, then? Well, when the sermon has reached a certain intensity, he might simply go into a kind of chant: "I want to tell you about my Jesus, yes, and how my Lord has come to me." His voice has lifted above its normal speech range and he is singing. He can no longer contain what his preaching has built up inside him. He cannot communicate what he is feeling by simply putting together subjects and predicates. He has to go beyond. He has to make that step.

Taking my people back home

Perhaps some readers saw the television show, "Like It Is," when it went to Andrew Young's home in Atlanta to ask him about his new position as the United States Ambassador to the United Nations. Most of the program was a very calm and matter-of-fact discussion about the new role and its duties and what he hoped to bring to it. At the end of the program they switched to a farewell service in his church, because Young is an active ordained minister.

There are a number of phrases in common use in the Black community which have come to mean much more than the literal meaning of the words. The phrases seem to us as old as time. We have heard them spoken at crucial moments of life as long as we can remember. By the saying of one of those phrases, people are transported to what we call "home." Such a phrase makes one feel safe, feel good, if only for a little while.

One of those familiar phrases has to do with trusting in the Lord. It evokes feelings of God's almighty care, God's love for me, no matter what is out there, no matter how tough things might get. God is going to take care of it. So what I've got to do is learn to trust in the Lord, and he will make a way.

In that closing, church scene on the television show, Andrew Young was talking to his congregation in a way that made the love between them almost tangible. He said: "I think that Jimmy Carter will make a fine president because I think he's a fine man. But I'm not going to put all my faith and trust in Jimmy Carter, because Jimmy Carter is a human being and human beings make mistakes. What I'm going to do is put my trust in the Lord."

I was watching the show hundreds of miles away, but I swear I could feel something that was taking place there, something going on between him and his congregation. He continued: "You know, I think the people in Congress are fine people, but I'm not going to put all my trust in the Congress. Because the Congress is made up of human beings and human beings can make mistakes. No, I'm going to put my trust in the Lord."

And again: "You know, the people at the U.N. are fine people, too, but I'm not going to put all my faith and trust in the people at the U.N., because the people at the U.N. are human beings and, like you and me, they make mistakes. I'm going to put my trust in the Lord."

And again: "I'm not even going to put all my faith in me. I'll try to do the best job I can, but I know that I am weak and I can fail. I'm going to put my trust in the Lord." I said to myself, "Now he's going to sing." While he was saying those last words, someone had started to play softly and one could feel that something was beginning to happen in that church.

The point is that no one had to stand up and announce: "We are beginning the preparation of the altar and gifts, so let's sing hymn number 47." Such an announcement would have been not only inappropriate and ridiculous but also entirely superfluous.

Music to help get it out

Instead, just as Young was repeating again that he was going to put all his trust in the Lord, he put his hands on the lectern, closed his eyes, and began to sing: "I'm going to trust in the Lord." And that did it. At that moment, the whole assembly rose to its feet and started singing. Andrew Young had no place else to go but to song at that point. He had to sing in order to get what was inside out, because he was feeling it with such intensity that the mere saying of words would have been totally inadequate.

If this is true for highly articulate people, it is even more true for others. I know a young woman in my neighborhood who has great difficulty with verbal communication. Her academic education was extremely limited and her environment and contacts with other people have been very limited, too. If she were to try to describe a family problem or a trauma in her life, her shyness coupled with her lack of talent for verbalizing would make the effort to communicate ineffectual, to say the least.

But I have heard her sing in her church. Immediately after a particularly tragic event had taken place in her life, I heard her sing at a service, "I Stood on the Banks of the Jordan," and then she sang "Precious Lord" ("take my hand, lead me on, help me stand, I am tired, I am weak, I am worn"). When she finished the song, the assembly sat in absolute silence. She had reduced the people to speechlessness, because this girl who could not articulate had communicated her own heaviness and tragedy so well in song.

The people did not know the nature of her trouble, but they knew without a doubt that one of their sisters was in trouble. After the service, the minister approached her, put his arm around her, and said something like, "I don't know what it is, honey, but the Lord will make a way. Trust in him." And the elders and some of the sisters of the congregation gathered around her and comforted her. She had got through to all of them more effectively and affectively than any smooth-tongued orator.

Once I saw an old woman, bent over with years of growing up and living Black and poor in America, walking tired and slow and stooped into a church where they celebrated a service that was out of sight. At the end of the service they sang, "I'm So Glad Jesus Lifted Me." When I looked over at the old woman, she had noticeably straightened up. She walked out of that church after the song with her head held high and her shoulders back. She was literally — literally — uplifted and glad and healed.

Some of us Catholics were trained to think of the presence of Christ among us in terms of transubstantiation and the words of consecration at mass. Some of us even know clergy who were so superstitious about those words and so scrupulous that they went to ridiculous lengths to make absolutely sure they were said just right.

In the Black church tradition, how do we know Jesus is with us? How do we know Jesus has arrived? We can feel him when he comes. And how do we get him here? By singing the words of the Lord, by praying and by putting our prayer into song, by singing and getting the spirit and beginning to feel what it is all about. And then somebody might begin to shout. People will move back and forth. They'll clap their hands. The singing will build and build and build, and people will know as surely as anyone ever could that Jesus is here.

The music proves itself

Therefore, when we are planning liturgies, we have to get away from the idea — put it behind us — that music is something to add a little sparkle to an otherwise dull worship experience. That approach makes no sense at all in terms of Black tradition. Music is not a lubricant that makes it easier to tolerate a liturgy that remains extrinsic to it. It is part of the stuff and heart of liturgy itself.

And there are other dangers and mistakes to be avoided, if we would learn from the Black tradition and experience. Our use of choirs must never be such that it invites the congregation to return again to audience status. Choirs are always used as back-ups for the whole community, so that everyone is about the business of praising the Lord in song.

Nor should we attempt to "make gospel music serious" by digging out the most complicated things that the Fiske Jubilee Singers ever did and deciding that those and those alone will be "good" Black music. Nor can we get anywhere by using anything (however good it is in itself) with the attitude that we are thereby "doing something for those people." If we can't do something for ourselves, if we can't enter into it, if we can't experience the thing we are doing, we should forget it.

I have done workshops in a great many parishes all over this country. I did one in Washington in a parish that had been labeled as the most conservative Black parish in the city. Well-meaning friends came to me in horror when they heard about the invitation. "Listen," they said, "don't do it. They'll drain you. They'll just drain you. There will be nothing left of you." But all this just made me want to go there even more — another challenge.

When I arrived, there was some evident resentment and some fear. "What is he here to do?" Well, I talked about what I was going to do. And the next day we spent a lot of time singing. And the last day we celebrated mass. The church was full, and I was nervous at seeing all those old Black folks. You have *never* been bawled out until you have been bawled out by old Black folks.

We sang familiar, traditional gospel hymns and we had a soloist do "Precious Lord." I knew that many of the families represented in that congregation had grown up on those hymns. But then they had become Catholics. And somewhere along the line they had decided that in order to be "good Catholics" they would have to "rise above" all that.

There was one old woman at mass who must have been in her nineties. She could hardly see and she could hardly walk. After communion, when the soloist was singing, I looked over at her and she was crying. When the celebration was over, most of the old Black women came over to me and were saying, "Well, son, it's about time. Why, we sang those songs years ago. Let me show you how we used to sing this one. It's about time."

I fear it was not because I or my presentation had been irresistible. It was because I merely reintroduced to those people something that was already in them. When some of their fears had been laid to rest, they were able to enter into the music as naturally and as beautifully as if they had been doing it all along. Later someone confided to me: "Do you know what some of them have been doing? They've been coming to mass on Sunday mornings and 'going to church' on Sunday afternoons."

What that whispered statement meant was that they were going across the street on Sunday afternoons to a Black Baptist church and finding that which they needed to survive. How long must we Catholics conduct ourselves and our parishes in such a way that part of our family has to run away from home to be revived?

AUTHORS

Henry H. Mitchell: The Reverend Dr. Henry Mitchell is Director of the Ecumenical Center for Black Church Studies of the Los Angeles Area; and Adjunct Professor at the American Baptist Seminary of the West (Berkeley and Covina), Fuller Theological Seminary of Pasadena, and the School of Theology at Claremont. He holds degrees from Lincoln University, Pennsylvania; Union Theological Seminary, New York City; California State University in Fresno (M.A. in linguistics); and the School of Theology at Claremont (Th.D. in Culture and Communication). He has served as a local pastor, a college instructor, a dean of chapel, and as the first Martin Luther King, Jr. Memorial Professor of Black Church Studies at Colgate Rochester/ Bexley Hall/Crozer. He is the author of *Black Preaching* (Lippincott, 1970) and *Black Belief* (Harper & Row, 1975). His 1974 Lyman Beecher Lectures on Preaching, delivered at Yale Divinity School, are the basis of his latest book, *The Recovery of Preaching,* to be published by Harper & Row this year.

Cyprian Lamar Rowe: Dr. Cyprian Lamar Rowe, F.M.S., is the Assistant Director of Pan-African Studies and Assistant Professor in Pan-African Studies, Humanities, at Temple University in Philadelphia. A Marist brother, he has studied at the City University of New York, spent two years as a research fellow at the University of Ghana, and earned his Ph.D. in African Studies at Howard University, Washington, D.C. Dr. Rowe is also a poet and has published poetry and essays in *Freeing the Spirit, Black World, First World* and *Liturgy.* Most recently he has been awarded a scholarship in the study of Clinical Social Work at Bryn Mawr.

William B. McClain: The Reverend William B. McClain is pastor of Union United Methodist Church, Boston, Massachusetts, and instructor in Black theology and the history of the Black church at Boston College. He has an A.B. from Clark College, Atlanta, Georgia; an M.A. in Education from Suffolk University, Boston; a Master of Divinity from Boston University; and he has completed his course work for a Ph. D. in Systematic Theology at Boston University.

Clarence Jos. Rivers: The Reverend Clarence Jos. Rivers is a priest of the Archdiocese of Cincinnati and head of Stimuli, Inc. (Cincinnati), consultants for the application of the performing arts and mixed media in the areas of education and celebration. He is a musician, widely known for his compositions and for workshops in song and liturgical music. Fr. Rivers is the author of *Soulfull Worship,* published by The National Office for Black Catholics in 1974, former editor of NOBC's magazine, *Freeing the Spirit,* and a dramatist whose musical play, *Turn Me Loose,* is based on the life of Frederick Douglass. Articles of his have appeared in The Liturgical Conference's membership journal, *Liturgy,* in March 1976 (an expanded version of the address contained in this volume) and in February 1977.

James P. Lyke: The Reverend James Patterson Lyke, O.F.M. is a Franciscan priest (Order of Friars Minor) and pastor of St. Thomas Church, Memphis, Tennessee. His A.B. is from Quincy College, Illinois, and his Master of Divinity in theology is from the Antonianum, Rome, through St. Joseph's Seminary, Teutopolis, Illinois. Fr. Lyke holds memberships in the Board of

Directors, Memphis NAACP; National Black Catholic Clergy Caucus; Advisory Board of The National Office for Black Catholics Department of Culture and Worship; Board of Trustees, The Catholic Theological Union (Chicago); NCCB Committee for the National Catechetical Directory; Diocesan Board for the Permanent Diaconate; and the Board of Directors, Beale St. Repertory Theatre. Formerly he was a member of the Board of Directors of The Liturgical Conference, of the Ad Hoc Committee on Priestly Life and Ministry of the NCCB, of the UFO Memphis Grape Boycott Committee, and was chairman of the Memphis Area Project South, an OEO delegate agency.

Edward K. Braxton: The Reverend Edward Braxton is a priest of the Archdiocese of Chicago, and the 1976-77 visiting lecturer in the William A. Coolidge Chair of Ecumenical Relations at Harvard University, Divinity School. Fr. Braxton's B.A., M.A., S.T.B. and S.T.L. degrees are from the Pontifical Faculty of Saint Mary of the Lake Seminary, Mundelein, Illinois. He holds a Ph.D. in Religious Studies and an S.T.D. in systematic theology from the Pontifical Faculty of the Catholic University of Louvain, Belgium. He was granted the theology doctorate *summa cum laude* for a dissertation entitled "Images of Mystery: A Study of the Place of Myth and Symbol in the Theological Method of Bernard Lonergan." Since his ordination in 1970, he has worked in parish and campus ministry, in retreats and lecturing, in adult education and teaching. He has published in *Irish Theological Quarterly, Social Compass, Louvain Studies, Chicago Studies, The Critic* and *Liturgy 70.* His professional associations include The American Academy of Religion, The Catholic Theological Society of America and the Black Catholic Clergy Caucus.

William L. Norvel: The Reverend William L. Norvel, S.S.J. is a Josephite priest and pastor of St. Benedict the Moor Church, Washington, D.C. Educated in Pascagoula and Biloxi, Mississippi, at Epiphany Apostolic College in New-burgh, New York, and at St. Joseph's Seminary, Washington, D.C., he was ordained in 1965. He has taught in New Orleans, directed Josephite brothers at St. Joseph the Worker Training Center there, and directed programs at St. Joseph's Seminary, Washington, D.C. When he was appointed pastor in 1971, he was the only Black pastor of a Catholic church in Washington, D.C. and the second Black priest to hold such a position in that predominantly Black city. He is a member of the NAACP, the Black Catholic Clergy Caucus, and the Board of Directors of The Liturgical Conference. Recently he was chosen by the Board of Directors of the Secretariat for Black Catholics in Washington to be the recipient of a Community Action Award in recognition of outstanding service to the Black community in the promotion of Black awareness and the dignity of Black people.

Henry J. Offer: The Reverend Henry J. Offer, S.S.J., is a Josephite priest and pastor of St. Francis Xavier Church, Baltimore, Maryland. Graduating from Sacred Heart Seminary College in Detroit, he went to Newburgh, New York for his novitiate, to St. Joseph's Seminary, Washington, D.C. for theology, and was ordained in 1944. Currently he is also Chairman of X-C.E.L.L. Therapeutic Community Drug Program in Baltimore, member of the Board of Directors and Secretary of City-Campers, Inc., and publisher of the Baltimore Black Arts Calendar. Fr. Offer's previous work has included parish ministry, missions and street preaching in Texas, Detroit and Baltimore; direction of pastoral training for newly ordained Josephites and of the archdiocesan Urban Commission; and membership in the General Council, St. Joseph's Society.

Grayson W. Brown: Mr. Brown is a musician and composer whose "A Mass for a Soulfull People" has been published by North American Liturgy Resources. He is organist and choral director at St. Ann's Church, Brooklyn, New York. His music is in use in many parishes throughout the United States and his workshops on affective liturgy in the Black spiritual tradition are popular. He is the conductor of a Liturgical Conference workshop being offered beginning in 1977 entitled "Planning Music as an Integral Dimension of Liturgical Worship." He received a commission to compose music for the Black Heritage program of the 1976 Eucharistic Congress in Philadelphia. Author of "Liberation Liturgies," which appeared in *Freeing the Spirit* in 1974, he has written both for that magazine and for *Liturgy.*

What is NOBC?

The National Office for Black Catholics, established in July, 1970, is a national organization representing the 1,000,000 Black Catholics across the country. Its primary role is to be an advocate within the Catholic Church for Black Catholics and all Black people.

The idea for the National Office for Black Catholics came from Black Catholics all over the country and from all walks of life — priests, religious brothers and sisters and lay men and women. Its programs are planned and implemented in response to the needs which they have identified. In that sense, NOBC is a *service* organization.

Goals

Responding to the challenge given by Pope Paul VI, "to enrich the Catholic Church with your valuable and unique gift of Blackness which she (the church) needs — especially at this moment in her history," NOBC pursues the following goals:

1. To share with U.S. Catholics the rich religious, intellectual and cultural tradition of the Black community, and particularly of the Black Catholic community
2. To enable Black Catholics to assume a greater responsibility for and participation in the Catholic Church in the Black community
3. To assist Black Catholics and the church in general in making an effective contribution to the total Black community
4. To influence the Catholic Church in America to: a) recognize, take action and eradicate racism within its own structure, and b) assume a more forceful stand against racism in American society

Organizational Structure

NOBC is governed by a Board of Directors, representing priests, religious brothers and sisters, and lay men and women.

Affiliated Organizations

The National Office for Black Catholics is also an umbrella organization, supporting the programs and activities of the following affiliate organizations:

The National Black Sisters Conference (NBSC)
Concerned with deepening the spirituality and promoting unity and solidarity among Black religious women

The National Black Lay Catholic Caucus (NBLCC)
Provides lay men and women with tools in leadership training on the parish level, community organizing and technical assistance

The National Black Catholic Clergy Caucus (NBCCC)
Composed of priests, brothers, deacons and members of the National Black Seminarians' Association (a component organization) — with major concerns in religious formation and proper training for pastoral ministry in the Black community

Support of Catholic Bishops

NOBC is endorsed by the National Conference of Catholic Bishops (NCCB). The NCCB maintains an Ad Hoc Committee for liaison with NOBC, representing it before the Catholic Bishops of America. The National Office for Black Catholics is listed in *The Official Catholic Directory.*

A Sense of Ownership

All Black Catholics throughout the United States can have a real sense of pride and ownership in the work of the National Office for Black Catholics. Over 65% of the operating budget for the National Office for Black Catholics is provided by them.

The BLACK CATHOLICS CONCERNED appeal reaches out to the one million Black Catholics of this country each year. By their generous response, Black Catholics form an effective coalition for furthering our concerns in the church and community. An additional 15% of NOBC's finances come from other concerned Catholics who are supportive of the goals and objectives of the National Office for Black Catholics. Several dioceses, recognizing the important contribution which NOBC is making to the total church, have extended the BLACK CATHOLICS CONCERNED appeal to all of their parishes. NOBC sincerely appreciates this support. The remaining money is obtained through grants designed for programs in the areas of education, vocation recruitment and lay leadership training.

The Core Staff

The staff of the National Office for Black Catholics is headed by an Executive Director. Other members of the staff are an administrative secretary, a receptionist, and program directors for *Culture and Worship Services, Public Relations,* and *Church Vocations.* NOBC's primary responsibility is to *identify, plan* and *implement* programs which are of service to the Black Catholics, the personnel serving the church in the Black community, and Black people in general.

Publications

The following resources may be obtained through The National Office for Black Catholics, 1234 Massachusetts Ave., N.W., Suite 1004, Washington, D.C. 20005 (prices subject to revision):

Freeing the Spirit, quarterly magazine, $10 per year
Impact, newsletter, $3.50 per year
This Far by Faith — American Black Worship and Its African Roots, $7.95
Soulfull Worship, by Clarence Jos. Rivers, $8.95
Doin' Jesus, booklet
Thinking of a Career (Women), booklet
Thinking of a Career (Men), booklet
Black Perspectives on Evangelization of the Modern World, booklet
Special Statement: The Crisis of Catholic Education in the Black Community, leaflet

THE LITURGICAL CONFERENCE

What Is The Liturgical Conference?

The Liturgical Conference is a voluntary nonprofit association of Christians, chiefly in the United States and Canada, who belong to different churches and confessional traditions but who have a common interest and concern: seeking to help all the churches celebrate public worship (liturgy) in ways that will express and nourish the faith community and that will speak to human needs.

Beginning in 1940 as an association of Roman Catholics, The Liturgical Conference has been since then and continues to be an educational, a motivating, and an advocacy force in Christian renewal, holding to the central and key role of liturgy in any faith community — but never in isolation from the general formation and education of that community, its mission, its witness to social justice and peace.

The Liturgical Conference endeavors to express needs that people feel and, with the help of all its members, tries to share the resources and experience that correspond to those needs. Anyone who shares its concerns for liturgical authenticity and vitality is eligible for membership, at $25 per year, which includes a subscription to its bimonthly membership journal, *Liturgy.*

Members of The Liturgical Conference elect a board of directors (three year term; one-third of the directors elected each year), which meets semiannually to set the policies of the association and to approve its projects. Its office and staff are located at the address below in Washington, D.C., implementing Conference projects and serving members' needs.

Further information as well as the resources listed below can be obtained from The Liturgical Conference, 1221 Massachusetts Ave., N.W., Washington, D.C. 20005 (prices subject to revision):

Periodicals

Liturgy, bimonthly journal for members of The Liturgical Conference (see above)

Homily Service — An Ecumenical Resource for Sharing the Word, $31/year

Living Worship, monthly, ten times a year, $6/year

Books

(unless "kit," "packet," or cassette is indicated)

This Far by Faith — American Black Worship and Its African Roots, $7.95

The Spirit Moves — A Handbook of Dance and Prayer, by Carla De Sola, $9.95

Strong, Loving and Wise — Presiding in Liturgy, by Robert W. Hovda, $8.25

Liturgy Committee Handbook, ed. by Virginia Sloyan, $5.25

The Lector's Guide, ed. by Gabe Huck and Virginia Sloyan, $4.75

The Ministry of Music, by William A. Bauman, $6.75. Companion cassette, $6.95. Combined book and cassette, $12.95

There Are Different Ministries — Guide for Acolytes, Ministers of Communion, Ushers and Occasional Ministers, by Robert W. Hovda, $4.95

From Ashes to Easter — Design for Parish Renewal (kit of materials for Lent as reinitiation for all), by Virginia Sloyan and Robert W. Hovda, $25

Major Feasts and Seasons (Vol. I: four packets for Advent, Lent, Summer and November [Saints, death, Thanksgiving] ; Vol. II: four packets for Christmastime, Eastertime, Festivals of Summer, and Autumn as a season of beginnings), by Gabe Huck, $55/volume

The Rite of Penance, Vol. I — Understanding the Document, by Ralph Keifer

and Frederick R. McManus, $7.00
The Rite of Penance, Vol. II — Implementing the Rite, ed. by Elizabeth McMahon Jeep, $7.25
The Rite of Penance, Vol. III — Background and Directions, ed. by Nathan Mitchell, o.s.b. (to be published Fall, 1977)
Parishes and Families — A Model for Christian Formation through Liturgy, ed. by Gabe Huck and Virginia Sloyan, $6.50
The Rites of People — Exploring the Ritual Character of Human Experience, by Gerard A. Pottebaum, $5.50
Dry Bones — Living Worship Guides to Good Liturgy, by Robert W. Hovda, $5.70
Simple Gifts — A Collection of Ideas and Rites from Liturgy, ed. by Gabe Huck, Vol. I and Vol. II, $5.00 each
Children's Liturgies, ed. by Virginia Sloyan and Gabe Huck, $10.25
Signs, Songs & Stories — Another Look at Children's Liturgies, ed. by Virginia Sloyan, $8.00
Manual of Celebration, by Robert W. Hovda, $12.00; *Supplement One,* $5.25; *Manual* and *Supplement* combined, $14.00
Celebrating Baptism, by Robert W. Hovda, 60¢

Meetings
North American Liturgical Week, annual three-day gathering of members and other interested persons: theme for 1977: "The Church as a Ministering Community"

Workshops
(available to local sponsors: dioceses, churches, groups)
Planning Music as in Integral Dimension of Liturgy — Mr. Grayson W. Brown
Presiding in Liturgy — Rev. Robert W. Hovda
Preaching from the New Lectionary — Rev. Hoyt L. Hickman
Proclaiming the Word: The Lector's Role — Rev. Gerard S. Sloyan
Sharing Sunday's Scriptures (Method for Group Process) — Ms. Mary C. Maher
Children's Liturgies — Ms. Elizabeth McMahon Jeep
Storytelling for Worship — Robert Bela Wilhelm, Th.D.
Celebrating the Major Feasts and Seasons of the Year — Mr. Gabe Huck
The Liturgy of the Hours in Parish and Religious Life — Rev. Andrew Ciferni, o.praem.
The Spirit Moves — A Workshop in Dance and Prayer — Ms. Carla De Sola
Environment and the Visual Arts in Worship — Mr. Frank Kacmarcik, Mr. Robert Rambusch, or Rev. Mr. Willy Malarcher
Liturgy Committees: The Art of Planning Good Liturgical Worship — Mr. Gabe Huck or Rev. G. Thomas Ryan
From Ashes to Easter: Design for Parish Renewal — Rev. Robert W. Hovda